THOMAS JEFFERSON AND

THE DEVELOPMENT OF

AMERICAN PUBLIC EDUCATION

JEFFERSON MEMORIAL LECTURES

Thomas Jefferson
and the
Development
of American Public
Education

By JAMES B. CONANT

University of California Press

BERKELEY AND LOS ANGELES

1963

UNIVERSITY OF CALIFORNIA PRESS

BERKELEY AND LOS ANGELES

CALIFORNIA

CAMBRIDGE UNIVERSITY PRESS

LONDON, ENGLAND

Preface

The three chapters of this book are based on three lectures which I had the privilege of giving at the University of California in March, 1960, under the terms of an endowment which provides for an annual series of Jefferson Memorial Lectures. The faculty committee had suggested that I speak on the general topic of the Jeffersonian tradition in American education. I gladly agreed, as my addressing an academic audience in Berkeley on this subject would be in the nature of a return engagement. Exactly twenty years earlier, as the Charter Day speaker I had taken as the title of my remarks "Education for a Classless Society: the Jeffersonian Tradition." At that time, as President of Harvard University I was much concerned with an enlarged scholarship program not only at Harvard but throughout the nation. Therefore, my references to Thomas Jefferson's ideas were largely determined by my own preoccupation with the need of introducing more social mobility into American society by means of a selective scholarship scheme.

Being faced with the responsibility of delivering these three lectures, I realized I must consider the whole range of the educational ideas of the most versatile of the founding fathers of the republic. My attempt to do so is recorded in the first and second chapters. In the third chapter I revert to my initial interest in one of Jefferson's original ideas, namely, the providing of opportunity for *free* education at all levels for carefully selected boys without funds. In order to do justice to Jefferson's many contributions to the development of American educational thought, however, I found it necessary to trace briefly the course of the development of our present pattern of public education. The second half of the volume, therefore, is in a sense my interpretation of the basic elements of American education. To those who are familiar with the details of the whole story, my history of the growth of American schools will appear far too brief, I am sure. But for readers who have little or no acquaintance with the history of American education, what I have put in print may perhaps prove a stimulus to further study. At least such is my hope. For important as it is for Americans to comprehend the greatness of Thomas Jefferson and to appreciate the originality of his thought, it is even more important for all citizens at this time to appreciate how our unique system of public education has evolved.

A number of the books to which I make reference in the notes are not easily available. I am indebted to the authorities in charge of the University of California Library at Berkeley, California, and the New York Public Library for their help and kindness. I am particularly indebted to Mrs. Margaret D. Uridge in Berkeley and to Mr. Gilbert A. Cam in New York, and for the facilities provided in the Frederick Lewis Allen Room of the New York Public Library.

Extracts from the following books are reprinted by permission:

Julian P. Boyd, ed., *The Papers of Thomas Jefferson* (Princeton, N.J.: Princeton University Press, 195–).

Saul K. Padover, ed., *The Complete Jefferson* (New York: Duell, Sloan and Pearce, 1943).

Roy J. Honeywell, *The Educational Work of Thomas Jefferson* (Cambridge, Mass.: Harvard University Press, 1931).

Lester J. Cappon, ed., *Adams-Jefferson Letters* (Chapel Hill, N.C.: University of North Carolina Press, 1959).

JAMES B. CONANT

New York

Significant Dates in the

Life of Thomas Jefferson

1743   Born at Shadwell, Albemarle County, Virginia, April 2
1760   Entered William and Mary College, March
1762   Graduated from William and Mary College, April
1767   Admitted to the Virginia bar
1769   Elected a member of the House of Burgesses of Virginia
1772   Married Martha (Wayles) Skelton, January
1775–1776   Member of the Continental Congress
1776–1779   Member of the House of Delegates of Virginia; reported educational reform bills
1779–1781   Governor of Virginia
1782   Mrs. Jefferson died, September
1783   Member of the Continental Congress
1784   Appointed as a negotiator to assist Benjamin Franklin in Paris, May
1785–1789   United States Minister to France
1790–1793   Secretary of State
1794–1796   In retirement at Monticello
1797–1801   Vice-President of the United States
1801–1809   President of the United States
1809   Again in retirement at Monticello, March
1814   Elected Trustee of Albemarle Academy
1816–1818   Made second attempt to establish a system of schools in Virginia
1818   Bill authorizing a state university passed by Virginia legislature, February 21
1818   Report of Commissioners to fix a site for the university (Rockfish Gap Report), August
1819   Rector of the University of Virginia
1825   University of Virginia opened, March
1826   Died at Monticello, July 4

Contents

Contents

I

Jefferson as an Educational Innovator

ALMOST EVERYONE who speaks or writes about Thomas Jefferson is certain sooner or later to refer to the inscription on his tombstone, which Jefferson himself composed. It reads as follows: "Here was buried Thomas Jefferson, author of the Declaration of Independence of the Statute of Virginia for religious freedom and Father of the University of Virginia."

More than one writer has been struck by the concluding words and has expressed surprise that a statesman of world renown, the third President of the United States, and the leader of a successful political party should have placed so high a value on the founding of a university. Why did Jefferson pick out from all his important undertakings and significant contributions his activities on behalf of the University of Virginia? Granted that in his old age the establishment of this institution became a cherished project, why did he consider this triumph in the field of education worthy of listing with the Declaration of Independence? Was it because he prized so highly the idea of a university and attached so much significance to the labor of academic men?

One is tempted to say the answer to the question is so obvious that the question itself is foolish. Clearly Jefferson had the highest regard for the mission of a university and that is reason enough, one is inclined to say, for his pride in the part he played in establishing the University of Virginia. Indeed, such a statement comes almost automatically from those of us who have spent our lives in institutions of higher education. And we are inclined to go on and wrap the mantle of Jefferson about us when we become eloquent in defense of universities in general or argue for support for some particular institution. The temptation is great, and at first sight the facts seem to support the contention, for Jefferson, in his later years, was more concerned with founding a university than with any other private or public undertaking. Yet a consideration of what Jefferson wrote about education both as a young man and late in life makes it quite evident that for him, a true university in Virginia was essential only because it was to be part of a total plan. And it was to the total plan that Jefferson gave his complete allegiance, as well he might, since the plan was his own invention. And just how novel and far-reaching was the invention will be evident, I hope, as I proceed.

In the first draft of his education proposal put forward in 1778–1779, the College of William and Mary was to be remodeled to provide what Jefferson believed to be required in the way of a university. The college and its friends did not take kindly to the idea, and this part of the project was abandoned; another way of providing advanced instruction in Virginia had to be found. Eventually it was found by the establishment of the state-supported university by the legislature in 1818, to be described in the next chapter. In the intervening thirty-nine years, however, the rest of the plan had fared no better than the proposal to remake a private college. Free schools in Virginia had not prospered. Quite the contrary. Even providing free elementary education for all was not an accomplished fact during Jefferson's lifetime.[1] So it was as a continually defeated educational reformer that Jefferson contemplated the final achievement of a portion of his original project. One can almost hear him exclaiming in the last years of his life, "At least the last stage is now a reality. The total plan must someday be put in operation," for Jefferson was an optimist to the end.

Thus, if my interpretation of Jefferson as an educational innovator is correct, his reference to the University of Virginia in the epitaph he wrote for his own tombstone points to an unfulfilled educational ideal for which he had argued without success for more

2

than forty years. The reference is clear evidence that the author of the Declaration of Independence put the highest value on education, but the total record shows that it was education as a whole that he constantly had in mind. He was concerned throughout his life, as in the first years of the Revolution, with education for everyone irrespective of family wealth or status, and his educational plan was part and parcel of his revolutionary political thinking. He envisaged the commonwealth of Virgina as a model republic, socially and politically different from any society in the past. To that end he envisaged a new educational pattern composed of several parts.[2]

First of all, free elementary schools were to be provided for all future citizens. Second, free education of a more advanced nature was to be provided for a selected group of poor boys through a series of residential grammar schools which were also to serve the well-to-do on a tuition basis. The selective process was to proceed in stages over a period of years. Third, a university education was to be provided at public expense for a selected few who would benefit from this education and who would, by virtue of this education, be ready to serve the state. Fourth, a true university was to be established in the state to accommodate this last group of students and others who were adequately prepared and could afford to pay. Such, in brief, are the four objectives of Jefferson's original plan for free schools in Virginia—his four proposals. But let Jefferson speak for himself. The earliest account of his educational proposal of 1779 (apart from the bill itself) is contained in a book published while Jefferson was in Paris in 1785 but written to a considerable extent while he was in retirement in 1781. The book is entitled *Notes on the State of Virginia* and in itself is a remarkable document showing the versatility of the interests of the writer, who describes for a French acquaintance the cultural, geographical, political, and social features of his native state. As to the bill for educational reform introduced into the legislature in 1779, Jefferson writes as follows:

This bill proposes to lay off every county into small districts of five or six miles square, called hundreds, and in each of them to establish a school for teaching reading, writing, and arithmetic [elementary schools]. The tutor to be supported by the hundred, and every person in it entitled to send their children three years gratis, and as much longer as they please, paying for it.[3]

3

Here is the enunciation of what I shall call Jefferson's first principle—free elementary education for all. It will be noted that these schools are to be so located as to be within walking distance of all the families; the one-room district school of the nineteenth century was similar in organization and intent.

Jefferson then proceeded to outline his second proposal for free selective education as follows:

These schools [the elementary schools] to be under a visitor who is annually to choose the boy of best genius in the school, of those whose parents are too poor to give them further education, and to send him forward to one of the grammar schools, of which twenty are proposed to be erected in different parts of the country, for teaching Greek, Latin, geography, and the higher branches of numerical arithmetic. Of the boys thus sent in one year, trial is to be made at the grammar schools one or two years, and the best genius of the whole selected, and continued six years, and the residue dismissed. By this means twenty of the best geniuses will be raked from the rubbish annually, and be instructed, at the public expense, so far as the grammar schools go. At the end of six years' instruction, one-half are to be discontinued (from among whom the grammar schools will probably be supplied with future masters); and the other half, who are to be chosen for the superiority of their parts and disposition, are to be sent and continued three years in the study of such sciences as they shall choose, at William and Mary College, the plan of which is proposed to be enlarged, as will be hereafter explained, and extended to all the useful sciences. The ultimate result of the whole scheme of education would be the teaching of all the children of the State reading, writing, and common arithmetic [Jefferson's first principle]; turning out ten annually, of superior genius, well taught in Greek, Latin, geography, and the higher branches of arithmetic [Jefferson's second principle]; turning out ten others annually, of still superior parts, who, to those branches of learning, shall have added such of the sciences as their genius shall have led them to [Jefferson's third principle]; the furnishing of the wealthier part of the people convenient schools at which their children may be educated at their own expense. The general objects of this law are to provide an education adapted to the years, to the capacity, and the condition of everyone, and directed to their freedom and happiness.

Let me interrupt my presentation of Jefferson's own account of his educational proposals to call attention to some of the implications of the novel scheme which he proposed in 1779. By modern standards three years of free education seems like a modest proposal indeed, but the suggestion that *all* the children (rich and poor alike) should receive a common education gratis was a proposal far too radical to be accepted in Virginia in 1779 or for many, many years. Indeed, the next chapter will be largely devoted to the long struggle by which this same doctrine was finally accepted throughout the different states of the Union until the common school, free and tax-supported, became an essential element in American society.

Even more radical were Jefferson's next two proposals: selective free education through the grammar school for the sons of the *poor* and free university education to be provided for the doubly selected "ten others of still superior parts." The bill of 1779 provided for elementary schools in every small district, which were to be within walking distance of the homes. In addition, there were to be a series of residential grammar schools. Those who were to select the location of these schools were charged "that the situation be as central as may be to the inhabitants of the said counties, that it be furnished with good water, convenient to plentiful supplies of provision and fuel, and more than all things that it be healthy." (The quotation is from Sect. 9 of the bill of 1779, entitled "A Bill for the More General Diffusion of Knowledge.") Section 11 of the same bill stated that the grammar schoolhouse "shall contain a room for the school, a hall to dine in, four rooms for a master and usher, and ten or twelve lodging rooms for the scholars." Clearly a residential school was what Jefferson had in mind, and a further section of the same bill specified free board and lodging for those whose parents were too poor to give them further education, *provided* they were those chosen to proceed to the grammar school of the district. The pupil's quota of the expenses of the house, together with a compensation to the master or usher for this tuition, at the rate of twenty dollars a year, was to be paid by the treasurer quarterly on warrant from the auditors. Those who could afford it, however, were to pay for their grammar school education. The bill set forth that the costs of food and service should be "divided equally among all the scholars boarding either on the public or private expense. And the part of those who are on private expense, and also the price of their tuition due to the master or usher, shall be paid quarterly by the respective scholars, their parents, or guardians, and shall be recoverable . . . on motion in any Court of Record." [4]

5

Neither in the draft legislation nor elsewhere does Jefferson discuss what standards are to be maintained for the paying pupils in the grammar school. A rigorous selection of those from indigent families who are to be educated at public expense is arranged in great detail. The first selection of "some one of the best and most promising genius and disposition" from each of ten schools was to be made by the overseer responsible for the ten schools in question. He was to make the appointment in the presence of at least two of the three elected officials of the county (aldermen) and was to stand interrogations by these officials "either on their own motion, or on suggestions from the parents, guardians, friends, or teachers of the children, competitors for such appointment." And if the elected county officials were not satisfied, they had the right to veto the appointment and the overseer was to try again!

The rather elaborate scheme for making the choice of those poor boys who were to attend the residential grammar schools *without charge* makes clear that Jefferson was aware of the difficulties involved in any selective scheme of education, particularly in a country with a free and easy type of society still largely frontier in outlook. The selective procedure for the scholarship recipients was not to be at an end, however, when the overseer had done his duty and his choice had been ratified by the county officials. In each grammar school there was to be an annual

visitation . . . for the purpose of probation, . . . at which one-third of the boys sent thither by appointment of the said overseers, and who shall have been there one year only, shall be discontinued as public foundations, being those who, on the most diligent examination and enquiry, shall be thought to be the least promising genius and disposition; and of those who shall have been there two years, all shall be discontinued save one only the best in genius and disposition, who shall be at liberty to continue there four years longer on the public foundation, and shall thence forward be deemed a senior.[5]

One might designate these proposals as a scholarship scheme with heavy emphasis on competition, but more was yet to come. The last section of the bill provided that the visitors for one set of districts should choose from the publicly supported seniors in the grammar schools in that set of districts the "one among the said seniors, of the best learning and most hopeful genius and disposition, who shall be authorized by them to proceed to William and Mary College; there to be educated, boarded, and clothed, three years; the expense of which annually shall be paid by the Treasurer on warrant from the Auditors." [6] Note "educated, boarded, and clothed"; this was to be, indeed, a full scholarship for the fortunate recipient. In our own time such handsome provision for a selected student is only to be found in certain institutions for those with unusual athletic talent!

There were undoubtedly many objections to Jefferson's ideas about public residential grammar schools: the expense was probably sufficient to cause rejection of the scheme out of hand, and free board and tuition for a few highly selected poor boys was far too radical an idea for Jefferson's contemporaries. Indeed, only slowly did the American citizens who paid taxes come to recognize the importance of free schools, and when by the middle of the nineteenth century the idea had become an accepted part of our tradition, there were few proponents of free *selective* education for youth without means. The mood of the American people for many generations was inherently hostile to any notion of educating one group of children at public expense for a longer period of time than all the others. As I shall attempt to show in the last chapter, the doctrine of equality of status came in conflict with the notion of equality of opportunity, and only in our own time do we see the possibility of a fruitful compromise.

But I am getting ahead of my story. Let me return to Jefferson's own formulation of his ideas. He never repeated the striking phrase "the best geniuses will be raked from the rubbish annually," though he continually reverted to the basic idea. After all, when Jefferson wrote his *Notes on Virginia,* he had no notion that he would spend a large portion of his active life in public affairs and certainly did not envisage becoming the leader of a successful political party whose major appeal was to many of those whom he referred to in 1781 as "the rubbish."

I write "many" not "all" because until the second and third decades of the nineteenth century the right to vote was restricted in most states of the Union by a property qualification.[7] I must, therefore, resist the temptation to write that Jefferson as a politician was to become President of the United States by virtue of the votes of those he had once designated as "rubbish."

In our own time it has become so popular as to be commonplace to quote Jefferson. In so doing, it is easy to pounce on the use of a word like "rubbish" and pronounce Jefferson to be an aristocratic snob; or it is easy to avoid all reference to the part of his plan that called for generous scholarships for a few selected poor boys; the temptation is great to emphasize only his arguments in favor of universal education (conveniently forgetting it was only free *elementary* education he had advocated). Since it is my attempt in this first chapter to examine Jefferson's educational ideas with reference to the time when they were formulated, I shall endeavor to treat them as a whole, as I believe Jefferson did throughout his life, though as a man of public affairs he sometimes stressed one argument rather than another.

His selective scholarship principle he justified in the *Notes on Virginia* with reference to the need of the state as follows: "By that part of our plan which prescribes the selection of the youths of genius from among the classes of the poor, we hope to avail the State of those talents which nature has sown as liberally among the poor as the rich, but which perish without use, if not sought for and cultivated." [8] (One might note in passing an assumption here about the distribution of talent which reflects the homogeneity of the white population.) After thus restating the case for the selective idea, he goes on to say:

But of the views of this law none is more important, none more legitimate, than that of rendering the people the safe, as they are the ultimate, guardians of their own liberty. For this purpose the reading in the first stage, when *they* will receive their whole education, is proposed, as has been said, to be chiefly historical: History, by apprizing them of the past, will enable them to judge of the future; it will avail them of the experience of other times and other nations; it will qualify them as judges of the actions and designs of men; it will enable them to know ambition under every disguise it may assume; and knowing it, to defeat its views. In every government on earth is some trace of human weakness, some germ of corruption and degeneracy, which cunning will discover, and wickedness insensibly open, cultivate and improve. Every government degenerates when trusted to the rulers of the people alone. The people themselves therefore are its only safe depositories. And to render even them safe, their minds must be improved to a certain degree.

Now comes a curious argument in favor of universal suffrage. "The influence over government must be shared among all the people," declares Jefferson, and continues,

If every individual which composes their mass participates of the ultimate authority, the government will be safe; because the corrupting the whole mass will exceed any private resources of wealth; and public ones cannot be provided but by levies on the people. In this case every man would have to pay his own price. The government of Great Britain has been corrupted, because but one man in ten has a right to vote for members of parliament. The sellers of the government, therefore, get nine-tenths of their price clear. It has been thought that corruption is restrained by confining the right of suffrage to a few of the wealthier of the people; but it would be more effectually restrained by an extension of the right to such numbers as would bid defiance to the means of corruption.

At the time Jefferson wrote his *Notes on Virginia,* he had retired (temporarily) to Monticello after having completed his term as Governor of Virginia. The War of Independence was coming to a close. (The surrender at Yorktown occurred on October 19, 1781.) The treaty of peace with Great Britain lay ahead (September 3, 1783), and in the final conclusion of the peace the author of the Declaration of Independence played a significant part. Shortly after writing his notes about Virginia, Jefferson, as a member of the Continental Congress, was active in procuring the presence of enough delegates to ratify the peace treaty in January, 1784. In July of the same year, Jefferson sailed for France, where he was to remain until October, 1789, as representative of the United States.

During his stay in Paris, Jefferson corresponded about his education bill, which had made no progress in the Virginia legislature. Quotations from his letter of 1786 to George Wythe and one of the same year to General George Washington are often cited by those who wish to emphasize the importance of universal education.[9] Some of the phrases used are striking. For example, to Washington he wrote: "It is an axiom in my mind that our liberty can never be safe but in the hands of the people themselves, and that too of the people with a certain degree of instruction. This it is the business of the state to effect, and on a general plan." The letters, however, add little to the views expressed in Jefferson's *Notes on Virginia.*

On his return from Paris, Jefferson became immersed in the politics of the new republic, serving first as Secretary of State (1790–1793), then as Vice-President (1797–1801), and finally as President (1801–1809). During this period he seems to have done little if anything to promote his novel ideas about education. For example, I can find no record of his writing about the selective features of his plan of 1779. His interest in higher education I shall discuss in the next chapter. Yet indirectly, in two ways at least, he influenced the history of American education during this period. In the first place, as President and leader of the newly formed Republican party he was listened to throughout the nation, and his advocacy of free schools must have been widely known even if he made no converts to his Virginia plan. In the second place, his purely political activities in this crucial period of American history had a profound effect on the educational development of the new nation. Without attempting to evaluate the rights and wrongs of his quarrel with Alexander Hamilton and the justification for his suspicion of the anti-democratic bias of the Federalist party, I think it fair to say that the triumph of Jefferson's own party at the polls in 1800 determined the political climate of the United States for a generation. (One can speak of the triumph of Jefferson's own party because Jefferson, if not the founder of the Republican party, was its effective leader when it decisively defeated the Federalists in the election of 1800.) Jefferson's anti-aristocratic views were shared by his associates in the new party, who joined him in an optimistic belief in the possibility of a government "in the hands of the people themselves." These views pointed the way to the extension of the suffrage to all male adults, and this extension in turn led even conservatives to see the necessity for at least elementary education for all. In short, the Jeffersonian revolution of 1800, as it is sometimes called, set the stage for the subsequent development of a more democratic opinion, which in turn influenced the way people thought about their schools.[10]

In one other respect the success of Jefferson as a politician influenced American public education profoundly. Jefferson and his followers were highly suspicious of centralized government. This suspicion—one might almost say "hostility"—was transmitted to the party of General Andrew Jackson, which absorbed many former Jeffersonians and, in general, regarded itself as the party of the people. We shall see how, for several generations after Jefferson's death, this distrust of central government hampered the state authorities in the work of improving schools. Not that the characteristically American system of local control of public schools (today there are some 40,000 independent school boards) can be attributed to Jefferson, but the political success of Jeffersonian democracy was surely one important factor in the development. Jefferson himself was far from consistent in his attitude toward the relation of the state to education. His plan envisaged local schools, locally controlled and supported largely by local taxes. Yet the scholarships for his selected few in the residential grammar schools and the university were to be supported by state funds. Furthermore, he had no objection to using the power of the state to remake the College of William and Mary or—when this idea was abandoned—to establish a state university.

The ambiguity in Jefferson's thought concerning the relation of the state to parents and children is well illustrated by what he wrote about compulsory education some ten years after his political career was over. In September, 1817, he sent a draft of "An Act for Establishing Elementary Schools" to his friend Joseph C. Cabell. In this bill it was provided (Sect. 6):

At this school shall be received and instructed gratis, every infant of competent age who has not already had three years' schooling. And it is declared and enacted, that no person unborn or under the age of twelve years at the passing of this act, and who is *compos mentis,* shall, after the age of fifteen years, be a citizen of this commonwealth until he or she can read readily in some tongue, native or acquired.[11]

In a footnote Jefferson discussed the "rights and duties of society towards its members, infant and adult." And he writes:

It is better to tolerate the rare instance of a parent refusing to let his child be educated, than to shock the common feelings and ideas by the public asportation and education of the infant against the will of the father. What is proposed here is to remove the objection of expense, by offering education gratis, and to strengthen parental excitement by the disfranchisement of his child while uneducated. . . . If we do not force instruction, let us at least strengthen the motives to receive it when offered.[12]

Jefferson appears to have obtained this idea of strengthening the "motives for education" from having read a copy of the Constitution of Spain proposed by the short-lived revolutionary Cortes in 1813 or 1814.

The author of the *Notes on Virginia* had been completely silent about compulsory attendance at school but had said that "the ultimate result of the whole scheme of education would be the teaching of all the children of the State reading, writing, and common arithmetic," which might be read to imply compulsory school attendance. At all events, thirty-odd years later, scruples about using the power of the state to coerce unwilling parents seem to have been prominent in his mind. A man who had created the Republican party and overthrown the Federalists on both the national and state levels might have more difficulty in advocating compulsory school attendance laws than had the young radical of 1779.

I have written "the young radical of 1779" because it is clear that for Jefferson a new type of education was part and parcel of a new type of political structure.[13] The most explicit evidence to support this interpretation of his views is contained in a letter he wrote in October, 1813, to John Adams about his efforts in Virginia at the time of the Revolution. In this famous letter he writes of the success he had had in persuading the first session of the Virginia legislature to pass laws abolishing entails and primogeniture, and then goes on to say,

These laws, drawn by myself, laid the axe to the root of Pseudo-aristocracy. And had another which I prepared been adopted by the legislature, our work would have been complete. It was a Bill for the more general diffusion of learning. . . . Worth and genius would thus have been sought out from every condition of life, and completely prepared by education for defeating the competition of wealth and birth for public trusts. . . . Although this law has not yet been acted on . . . I have great hope that some patriotic spirit will, at a favorable moment, call it up, and make it the keystone of the arch of our government.[14]

Thus we see that five years after he had left the Presidency and ceased to be the head of the great political party of the common man, Jefferson was still hoping that his original proposal of 1779—a selective system of free education—would be made the "keystone of the arch of our government." Yet, the record fails to show that in the days when he exercised great political power he did very much to make his scheme a reality. What is lacking is any evidence that he put the weight of his political influence when he still had it into forwarding his scholarship proposals or his scheme of residential grammar schools in either Virginia or any other state. Yet he did not withdraw his support of it. He was still loyal to his plan of 1779; in 1813 he was justifying it to John Adams as a measure necessary because of its sociological and political implications.[15] Jefferson's originality is manifest by the fact that almost alone among eighteenth-century thinkers he saw education as a social process.

What might be called Jefferson's second attempt to reform Virginia education was made in 1817. It was a consequence of his re-entry into the politics of education in his native state which started with his election to the board of trustees of Albemarle Academy on March 23, 1814. As one historian has written:

From that election dates the beginning of the actual development process of the Albemarle Academy into the University of Virginia. After long years of inquiry and reflection, Jefferson had evolved in his own mind a system of higher education, of which William and Mary had supplied the original germ. That system was now to be grafted upon Albemarle Academy and made to flourish under Jefferson's own eye.[16]

I postpone until the next chapter a consideration of how a private academy which existed only on paper was transformed into a university. I postpone also a discussion of the fate of Jefferson's proposal for elementary schools. In the remaining pages of this chapter I shall concentrate attention on the evolution of Jefferson's ideas about grammar schools and the selective features of his scholarship scheme of 1779.

Jefferson became a trustee of Albemarle Academy in March of 1814. In September of the same year he wrote a long letter to Peter Carr setting forth his views on education in general and raising the question as to what part in his comprehensive scheme might be played by Albemarle Academy. It is interesting to contrast in detail Jefferson's views as expressed in this letter and subsequent ones during the next few years with the ideas of the young Jefferson. Jefferson had been matured by a life rich in political experience; a new nation had been formed and prospered, and the Old World had been shaken by a revolution and the Napoleonic Wars. In Virginia, private academies had been started in a number of communities. Wealthy people were obtaining advanced education for their children through private schools up and down the Atlantic Coast. Considering the vast changes that had occurred since 1779, it is remarkable that Jefferson's basic ideas about education had been so little modified. We find in the letter of 1814 the outline of an ambitious plan for the entire state. The treatment of elementary schools is a repetition of his earlier proposals. However, the term "grammar schools" has now disappeared and the term "general schools" introduced. Of them he writes,

At the discharging of the pupils from the elementary schools, the two classes separate—those destined for labor will engage in the business of agriculture, or enter into apprenticeships to such handicraft art as may be their choice; their companions, destined to the pursuits of science, will proceed to the college, which will consist, 1st of general schools; and, 2d, of professional schools. The general schools will constitute the second grade of education.

The learned class may still be subdivided into two sections: 1. Those who are destined for learned professions, as means of livelihood; and 2. The wealthy, who, possessing independent fortunes, may aspire to share in conducting the affairs of the nation, or to live with usefulness and respect in the private ranks of life. Both of these sections will require instruction in all the higher branches of science; the wealthy to qualify them for either public or private life; the professional section will need those branches, especially, which are the basis of their future profession, and a general knowledge of the others, as auxiliary to that, and necessary to their standing and association with the scientific class. All the branches, then, of useful science, ought to be taught in the general schools, to a competent degree, in the first instance. These sciences may be arranged into three departments, not rigorously scientific, indeed, but sufficiently so for our purposes. These are, I. Language; II. Mathematics; III. Philosophy.[17]

The grammar schools have been transformed into general schools or colleges, and in this plan nothing is said about the selection of poor but able students to be educated at public expense. The old idea reasserts itself, however, in the draft legislation Jefferson sent to his friend Joseph C. Cabell in October of 1817. (This was the companion piece to a draft, sent in September of the same year, in which occurs the provision referred to that "every infant of competent age who has not already had three years' schooling" shall receive instruction gratis.) The second piece of proposed legislation which Jefferson sent to Cabell bore the title "A Bill for the Establishment of District Colleges and University"; the two drafts were combined under the title "A Bill for Establishing a System of Public Education." The "colleges" were the grammar schools of

1779 under a new name but now only nine in number rather than twenty. The commonwealth was to be divided into collegiate districts, each with its board of visitors, who were charged to choose a site for a college and arrange for the erection of

one or more substantial buildings—the walls of which shall be of brick or stone, with two school rooms, and four rooms for the accommodation of the professors, and with sixteen dormitories in or adjacent to the same, each sufficient for two pupils . . . to lodge, with a fireplace in each, and the whole in a comfortable and decent style, suitable to their purpose.[18]

The residential colleges, like the grammar schools in the bill of 1779, were to provide instruction in Greek and Latin. Also, instruction in modern languages (French, Spanish, Italian, German) was to be given. English grammar, geography, "the higher branches of numerical arithmetic, the mensuration of land, the use of the globes, and the ordinary elements of navigation" were likewise to be taught—a modified and modernized version of the grammar school curriculum, one might almost say. Gone is the rigorous provision for the elimination of the less able students among those who were supported by the state, but the last section of the bill (Sect. 42) provides for a selective process for the admission of poor but capable boys. It is provided that

the Visitors of the Ward-schools in every county [i.e., the local elementary schools] . . . after the most diligent and impartial observation and enquiry of the boys who have been three years at the Ward-schools, and whose parents are too poor to give them a collegiate education, shall select from among them some one of the most promising and sound understanding, who shall be sent to the first meeting of the Visitors of their collegiate district, with such proofs as the case requires and admits, for the examination and information of that Board; who, from among the candidates so offered from the several counties of their district, shall select two of the most sound and promising understanding, who shall be admitted to their College, and there maintained and educated five years at the public expense.[19]

The bill then goes on to provide that the collegiate visitors shall select "that one of the two who shall, on their most diligent and impartial inquiry and best information, be adjudged by them to be of the most sound and promising understanding and character, and most improved by their course of education, who shall be sent on immediately thereafter to the University." The one thus selected is then entitled to three additional years' education at public expense. The funds for this purpose as well as for supporting the poor boys in the college were to be provided by the state. Not only tuition but board and lodging appears to have been envisaged, as the words "publicly maintained" are used, but unlike the bill of 1779 nothing is said about clothing. The purpose of the draft legislation of 1817 Jefferson described as follows: "The object [of the bill] is to bring into action that mass of talents which lies buried in poverty in every country, for want of the means of development, and thus give activity to a mass of mind, which, in proportion to our population, shall be the double or treble of what it is in most countries." [20] A better statement in favor of a generous selective scholarship policy has never been written.

In spite of the eloquence of his letters, Jefferson's proposals of 1817 fared no better than those of 1779. As I shall explain in some detail in the next chapter, the crosscurrents of politics and differences of opinion among educational reformers resulted in little positive action by the Virginia legislature in 1817–1818. Jefferson's bill received only a few votes in the legislature (the House of Delegates) in February, 1818. But Jefferson remained active on behalf of the intermediate schools. In December, 1824, he wrote once again to Cabell. By this time he seemed ready to give up his principle of collegiate districts and urged the founding of colleges in the principal towns or the support of the academies already in existence in the towns. Honeywell writes,

Probably . . . he was consciously trying to make the plan attractive to the influential interests associated with each of these localities or institutions which had contributed to the defeat of his plan on earlier occasions. In the weariness of old age it seemed better to establish an imperfect plan than none and he caught eagerly at this unexpected opportunity to make a beginning.[21]

But Cabell replied that the proposal was too bold for existing public opinion. A last effort by Jefferson was made in the late winter of 1826, when an amended bill of 1817 was proposed in the House of Delegates but defeated. On July 4 of the same year, Jefferson died at Monticello, Virginia. No one undertook to continue his fight for a system of grammar schools or colleges. No one expressed interest in proposals to cull the "natural aristocracy of talents and virtue" and educate it "at the public expense, for the care of the public concerns." [22] The curtain had fallen on the lifelong effort of an educational innovator to persuade his fellow citizens of the importance of opening higher education to outstanding youth irrespective of family fortune.

I conclude this chapter by raising a question that should be answered by a professional historian. What were the sources of Jefferson's ideas about education? After his arrival in Paris in 1784, Jefferson was exposed to many influences from the Old World, and he in turn probably influenced the minds of some who were active in the French Revolution. After he became President of the United States, he was exposed to a variety of opinions about education. Jefferson's claim to fame as an educational innovator rests, however, not on what he wrote in his old age or even in middle life but what he wrote when he was not yet forty. The bill of 1779 and his *Notes on Virginia* express radical ideas about education as an instrument of republican policy. How did Jefferson happen to develop these ideas in colonial America of the 1770's? He certainly did not get them from England, as this was the period in which Oxford and Cambridge were at their lowest point, and the best education was provided in the academies of the dissenters who were debarred from the two ancient universities. Free elementary education had been introduced in Prussia as early as 1716 by Frederick William I and had been made thoroughgoing by a regulation of Frederick the Great in 1763.[23] News of this action by one of the great figures of the day probably reached Virginia and could conceivably have influenced Jefferson's views about universal free elementary education. The need for remaking William and Mary into a real university was almost obvious, but how did Jefferson come to conceive of his selective system for free scholars to be "raked from the rubbish" annually and educated at the "public expense" for the care of the public concerns?

Such evidence as there is points to Scotland as the source of Jefferson's thoughts about schools and universities.[24] If this be so, it is a strange paradox that Jefferson, a deist who had no sympathy with Calvin or the Calvinists and hated a theocracy, should have developed ideas which can be traced straight back to John Knox's *Book of Discipline of 1561.*

To be sure, I have no evidence that Jefferson had ever read the first *Book of Discipline,* in which Knox outlined an entire scheme of education, though we know he had a copy in his library.[25] While Knox's ideas were never fully implemented, the Scottish educational system during the first half of the eighteenth century was to some degree a reflection of his views. We know that Jefferson, while a student at William and Mary College, was much influenced by the Scottish professor of natural philosophy, moral philosophy, and mathematics, Dr. William Small. Jefferson saw a great deal of Small and was a frequent guest with him at Governor Fauquier's dinners, at which the range of conversation was, according to all reports, broad enough to have included education in Scotland. Above all, the bill on education drafted by Jefferson and reported by him to the Virginia Assembly in 1779 "for the general diffusion of knowledge" outlines a system of education that is strikingly similar to that of Knox.

Knox's plan called for the establishment of a school in each parish to supply elementary education for all boys up to the age of eight. Jefferson would have divided each county into hundreds, the size of which would have been regulated so that they would contain "a convenient number of children to make up a school" at which all free boys and girls would be "entitled to receive tuition gratis, for the term of three years." Knox would have sent those pupils who had demonstrated the capacity to benefit from more education to a grammar school for three or four years. Jefferson would have had the "best and most promising genius and disposition" from each group of hundred schools "proceed to the grammar school" for at least one year. At the end of that time, one-third of the boys would have been dropped, and after two years all would have been dropped "save only the best in genius and disposition," who would have been permitted to continue for four additional years "on the public foundation." Knox had also provided for this advanced grammar school education at institutions which he called "higher grammar schools or colleges." In both cases the really outstanding but poor boys would have been able to go on to higher education at the university level. Interestingly enough, Knox's scheme is more comprehensive than Jefferson's, in which the number of needy youth to be educated was strictly limited by political subdivision. Knox, on the other hand, emphasized that no scholar of ability was to be barred because of poverty from achieving the highest level of education of which he was capable. He arranged for a quarterly system of testing by "ministers and other learned persons" to decide whether a youngster should be maintained at school or should be sent to a trade. Jefferson had a similar system of examinations, but his were to be conducted by the official visitors of the school on an annual basis.[26]

Knox's scheme was a Presbyterian Church system first and foremost, and a state system only insofar as, for him, the church was the state. He proposed to pay for the schools from the funds obtained by the confiscation of the properties of the various establishments of the Catholic Church. The power of the nobles and the turbulence of Scottish politics prevented the fulfillment of such a grandiose proposal. Knox had in view advanced education of the most able for service to the state, as did Jefferson. But their two views of the ideal state were antithetical. Writing of John Knox and the Reformation, Andrew Lang [27] has said, "People who only know modern Presbyterianism have no idea of the despotism which the Fathers of the Kirk tried for more than a century to enforce." Knowing this history, both Small and Jefferson must have looked back with hatred to the Scottish Reformation. Yet Jefferson's mind was never closed. It was characteristic of him to pick up information and new ideas from any source, whether he thought well of it or not. Scotland in the first half of the eighteenth century was no theocracy, but the scheme outlined by the dogmatic Presbyterians was still to some degree in operation. Therefore, I offer to the reader my hypothesis that a sixteenth-century educational scheme put forward to perpetuate a spiritual tyranny became, through Jefferson's eighteenth-century alchemy, a grand innovation to secure religious freedom and personal liberty in the new republic overseas. It is characteristic of an innovator that he wields an almost magic pen.

2

The Fate of Jefferson's Proposals in the Nineteenth Century

I T WOULD BE pleasant if I could use this chapter to tell the reader of the success in the nineteenth century of Jefferson's new and bold educational ideas. But I cannot. Of the four objectives embodied in Jefferson's eighteenth-century proposals only the last, the establishment in Virginia of a true university, was realized in his lifetime. The first, the provision of free elementary education, was slowly accepted in principle but largely negated in practice. It was not until the 1860's that free public elementary education *for all* became a widely accepted doctrine in the United States. Of the second and third objectives—the selection of promising pupils from poor families for education in a residential grammar school and then in a university at public expense—we hear almost nothing throughout the long debates over schools and colleges which were a constantly recurring factor in the politics of every state. Indeed, the repudiation of what I shall call the Jeffersonian selective principle had become so complete in the United States that, when the renaissance of interest in Jefferson occurred in the twentieth century, the scholarship features of his plan were passed by in almost complete silence. To many, Jefferson's name was synonymous with universal free education. In short, his many eloquent statements in support of his first and fourth objectives were remembered and repeated; the rest of his plan was largely forgotten.[1]

This chapter will be devoted to a consideration of Jefferson's first and fourth objectives, namely, the provision of free elementary schools for all and the establishment of a true university in Virginia. I shall start with a brief discussion of the founding of the University of Virginia because, as I have already indicated, this is the one success in the field of education which Jefferson achieved during his lifetime. Furthermore, the foundation was important for the future of American higher education. Jefferson's part in it is of extreme significance to those who are primarily concerned with Jefferson's versatile personality and his mature views about matters cultural and intellectual. Since, however, my main concern is with the fate of Jefferson's total plan of education, I shall devote only a few pages to a subject on which chapters have already been written.[2]

In 1779 Jefferson proposed to make the College of William and Mary the capstone of the pyramid of education he was seeking to erect in Virginia. But he did not have in mind the college as it then existed and with which he was very familiar, having attended it from March, 1760, to April, 1762. Indeed, his attacks on his alma mater (he received the A.B. degree in 1762) place Jefferson in the company of distinguished but highly critical alumni! His criticisms appear to have stemmed in part from strong opposition to clerical tyranny of any sort. At the time he was a student, the professors were required to subscribe assent to the Thirty-nine Articles of the Church of England (a provision similar to that in force at Oxford and Cambridge from the time of the Restoration). Dr. William Small, the amazing Scot who had so much influence on Jefferson's youth, remained at the college for only six years (1758 to 1764) and left under circumstances that indicated that the Board of Visitors were less than interested in the development of the subject of natural philosophy. Small returned to England in 1764 to purchase some scientific apparatus for the college and decided not to return, apparently as a result of a clash with the Board of Visitors.

At this period, the College of William and Mary seems to have been running downhill rapidly. In 1729, there had been six professors on the faculty (the limit set by the charter), all of whom were graduates of Edinburgh, Oxford, or Cambridge. By 1766, however, Reverend John Camm, the professor of divinity, was the only person left to instruct those students who had completed their studies in the grammar school which was incorporated in the college. In his *Notes on Virginia*, Jefferson describes very briefly the origin of the college and its charter, which provided for "twenty visitors, who were to be legislators," and "a president and six professors." "After the present revolution," writes Jefferson in 1781, "the visitors having no power to change those circumstances in the constitution of the college which were fixed by the charter," undertook to change the objectives of the professorships. He also writes hopefully of the legislature's authorizing an increase in the number of professorships. He says nothing about his bill to amend the constitution of the college, which had been before the legislative assembly since 1779.[3] Perhaps he had already given up hope of a radical reformation, but it is worth noting what he had in mind originally for a university built out of William and Mary College.

The first section of the bill for the remaking of the college recites the history of the College of William and Mary at some length and in legislative language. The second section opens with a statement that must have been highly obnoxious to all loyal sons of the institution. It reads as follows:

And whereas the experience of near an hundred years hath proved, that the said College, thus amply endowed by the public, hath not answered their expectations, and there is reason to hope, that it would become more useful, if certain articles in its constitution were altered and amended,

and a few lines later continues,

and the late change in the form of our government [an understatement by the author of the Declaration of Independence, by the way] as well as the contest of arms in which we are at present engaged [the Revolutionary War was not yet over] calling for extraordinary abilities both in council and field, it becomes the peculiar duty of the Legislature, at this time, to aid and improve the seminary, in which those who are to be the future guardians of the rights and liberties of their country may be endowed with science and virtue, to watch and preserve the sacred deposit.[4]

22

After this rather long preamble, the bill reduces the number of visitors to five only, "who shall be appointed by joint ballot of both houses of Assembly, annually" and specifies many details about administrative officers which would not recommend themselves to either professors or administrators today. (The procedures were too cumbersome.) I suspect, however, that the main objection of the conservatives in Virginia to this bill is to be found by noting that the five visitors "shall not be restrained in their legislation . . . [by] the canons or the constitution of the English Church, as enjoined in the said charter [the charter then in force]." [5] In other words, Jefferson proposed to secularize a college closely connected with the Church of England. Later Jefferson attributed the failure of his bill in part to the opposition of the dissenters, who were afraid of an institution which had been so Episcopalian. Whatever the cause of the hostility, the measure was soon abandoned.

In the light of Jefferson's later ideas, the reform of the College of William and Mary he proposed in 1779 was hardly revolutionary. Six professors were to be increased to eight, one for each of the following subjects: one of moral philosophy, the laws of nature and nations, and the fine arts; one of law and police; one of history, civil and ecclesiastical; one of mathematics; one of anatomy and medicine; one of natural philosophy and natural history; one of the ancient languages, oriental and northern; and one of modern languages. The professorship of theology was to be abolished. Provision was made for a missionary to be sent by the professors "to the several tribes of Indians . . . to investigate their laws, customs, religions, traditions and more particularly their languages constructing grammar thereof." Such a provision, it might be claimed, was a forerunner to professorships in anthropology and modern linguistics.

By the turn of the century, Jefferson's acquaintance with the world of culture and learning had been enormously expanded. He had spent five years in Paris and had made many friends among the scholars and philosophers of the time, including the natural philosophers. In 1794 he had toyed with the idea of moving *in toto* the French faculty of the College of Geneva in Switzerland to the United States and setting them up as a university in Virginia.[6]

A letter of Jefferson's to Joseph Priestley, the famous English chemist and dissenter who had settled in America, dated January

18, 1800, illustrates the way Jefferson's thoughts about universities were developing:

We have in that State [Virginia] a College (William and Mary) just well enough endowed to draw out the miserable existence to which a miserable constitution has doomed it. . . . We wish to establish in the upper county [Jefferson's part of Virginia], and more centrally for the State, an University on a plan so broad and liberal and *modern,* as to be worth patronizing with the public support, and be a temptation to the youth of other States to come and drink of the cup of knowledge and fraternize with us. . . . I will venture even to sketch the sciences which seem useful and practicable for us, as they occur to me while holding my pen. Botany, chemistry, zoölogy, anatomy, surgery, medicine, natural philosophy, agriculture, mathematics, astronomy, geography, politics, commerce, history, ethics, law, arts, fine arts.[7]

In a subsequent letter he apologized for omitting languages, an obvious oversight.

At about this same time (1800) Jefferson became acquainted with the ideas of a French economist and philosopher, Pierre Du Pont de Nemours, whom he had known in Paris and who came to New York in early 1800. Du Pont de Nemours drew up a complete plan for a system of national education in the United States and published it in Paris.[8] The city of Washington was to be the site of four *grandes écoles,* which were to be the last stage in an all-inclusive national system starting with the common schools and involving intermediate colleges. The four *grandes écoles* were to be concerned with the following subjects: (1) medicine, (2) mining, (3) legislation, and (4) higher mathematics. Some writers are inclined to the opinion that Jefferson's ideas about university organization were much influenced by Du Pont de Nemours' volume. Certainly while he was President of the United States, Jefferson became increasingly interested in higher education and in 1806 supported a bill for the establishment of a national academy and university in the city of Washington, and district colleges throughout the nation.

In his sixth annual message (December, 1806) President Jefferson recommended an amendment of the Federal Constitution to legalize federal support of a national university. His words were far more cautious than those he had used in 1779 in proposing that the state reconstitute the College of William and Mary. "Education," he declared, is placed among the articles of public care, not that it would be proposed to take its ordinary branches out of the hands of private enterprise, which manages so much better all the concerns to which it is equal; but a public institution can alone supply those sciences which, though rarely called for, are yet necessary to complete the circle, all the parts of which contribute to the improvement of the country, and some of them to its preservation.[9]

Though nothing came of this Presidential recommendation—the bill for a national university died in committee—yet Jefferson's words are highly significant to anyone interested in the development of his thoughts over the years. By 1806, though Jefferson had led and dominated an anti-aristocratic party in opposition to the Federalists, we find him more than reconciled to leaving to private institutions the management of the ordinary branches of education.

In the letter to Peter Carr of 1814 (referred to in the previous chapter) and later in the report to the legislature of a committee of which he was chairman (Rockfish Gap Report, 1818), Jefferson went far beyond the modest proposals of 1779 for remaking the College of William and Mary.[10] A whole host of subjects were to be taught at the highest level. As a consequence, the Board of Visitors of the newly established university in 1824 provided for eight professors to head eight separate schools, each of which was to include in its scope a wide range of subjects. The significance of this arrangement lay in the fact that a student could study in one of the schools only, if he so desired. Thus, in a sense, Jefferson may be said to be the originator of the elective system. A letter of his to Professor George Ticknor of Harvard on July 16, 1823, is often quoted in support of his claim. In it Jefferson wrote:

I am not fully informed of the practices at Harvard, but there is one from which we shall certainly vary, although it has been copied, I believe, by nearly every college and academy in the United States. That is, the holding the students all to one prescribed course of reading, and disallowing exclusive application to those branches only which are to qualify them for the particular vocations to which they are destined. We shall, on the contrary, allow them uncontrolled choice in the lectures they shall choose to attend, and require elementary qualifications only, and sufficient age.[11]

I have sketched the evolution of some of Jefferson's ideas about higher education—ideas which had a profound effect on the development of collegiate instruction in the United States. Unless I am to turn this chapter into an account of the University of Virginia, I must briefly summarize the steps by which his dream of a university became a reality. Jefferson as a young radical had wanted a university as part of a total plan. And though his attention became more and more drawn to the final stage of education, he stuck to his original concept during his second attempt to reform education in Virginia, which began in 1814. He was forced to abandon all three of his first four objectives, however, when on February 11, 1818, his Bill for Establishing a System of Public Education was overwhelmingly defeated. He was ready to agree with his loyal friend Joseph C. Cabell, a member of the legislature, that a plan for a university without district colleges (or grammar schools) was better than none. So a bill was passed authorizing a state university on February 21, 1818.[12] The location as well as many other matters were still undetermined. The act required the governor to appoint a commission of twenty-four members to determine the site, the plan, the branches of learning to be taught, the number of professors, and the general provisions for organization. So came about a famous document in the history of higher education in the United States, the so-called Rockfish Gap Report, written by Jefferson as chairman.[13] The great issue to be settled by the commission when it met in August, 1818, was not a pedagogic one but a highly practical one. Where was the university to be located? Jefferson wanted it to be in his part of Virginia; indeed, he wanted it to be based on Albemarle Academy, recently transformed on paper into Central College. And it was. A master politician had his way with his fellow commissioners. The legislature was another story. Here the struggle was bitter, as geographical struggles in education usually are. On January 19, 1819, a bill embodying the report of the commission passed the House of Delegates, and on January 25, the Senate. Central College, once Albemarle Academy, became the University of Virginia.[14] Shortly thereafter Jefferson was appointed one of the visitors and, in the spring of the same year, rector of the university. He was then seventy-five years old. He dedicated his remaining seven years to the physical and spiritual planning of the university of which he proudly called himself the father.

Before proceeding further, I venture to call the reader's attention to the correspondence between Thomas Jefferson and the person who acted almost as his legislative agent, Joseph C. Cabell, a member of the Senate. Cabell was the practical politician who tried to get the legislature to act as Jefferson desired. The exchange of letters amply demonstrates that the functioning of political machinery as regards educational matters has changed but little in the course of the last 140 years. I omit reference to the letters concerned with the passage of the act establishing the university or those which dealt with the acceptance by the legislature of the Rockfish Gap Report. I shall be able to give the reader only a glimpse of the political problem of financing the construction of the buildings which Jefferson himself designed.

On February 11, 1822, Cabell wrote to Jefferson in some distress:

In my last I informed you that we then contemplated the plan of asking the legislature to give the University the surplus revenue of the literary fund [a state fund] to the amount of $7,200, which would be equivalent to the release of the debt . . . Mr. Johnson and myself had thought, by this expedient, we should get clear of the commitment of our friends in the House of Delegates against any scheme which would go to the diminution of the capital of the literary fund. To my great regret, however, I discovered that our friend, Mr. Morris of Hanover, Chairman of the Committee of Schools and Colleges, would not support the measure. . . . It being most clear that we could carry no measure in which the friends of the University should be divided, and it being in every way important to have the support of Mr. Morris, I was compelled to abandon the measure. . . .[15]

Subsequent attempts during the same session were no more successful. When the next session opened in December of the same year, Cabell wrote of the difficulties which appeared still to stand in the way of financing the construction of the buildings and seemed to indicate a possible temporizing or retrenchment. Jefferson replied in a long, vigorous letter, part of which reads as follows:

Of all things the most important, is the completion of the buildings. . . . The great object of our aim from the beginning, has been to make the establishment the most eminent in the United States, in order to draw to it the youth of every state, but especially of the south and west. We have proposed, therefore, to call to it characters of the first order of science from Europe, as well as our own country; and, not only by the salaries and the comforts of their situations, but by the distinguished scale of its structure and preparation. . . . Had we built a barn for a college, and log huts for accommodations, should we ever have had the assurance to propose to an European professor of that character to come to it? . . . To stop where we are, is to abandon our high hopes, and become suitors to Yale and Harvard for their secondary characters to become our first. . . . The report of Rockfish Gap, sanctioned by the Legislature, authorized us to aim at much higher things. . . . The opening of the institution in a half-state of readiness, would be the most fatal step which could be adopted. . . .[16]

To which Cabell replied on January 9, 1823:

I am happy to inform you that our prospects are now very favorable. Everything is understood; everything is arranged. Our bill will be introduced in the Committee of Schools and Colleges in a day or two. We ought to have had a select committee to get rid of enemies and to expedite; but the report was committed to the Committee of Schools and Colleges by a member who knew not our views, and there would be certain difficulties in getting it away from that committee. We hope we are strong enough to meet our adversaries at every stage. . . .[17]

Two weeks later on January 23 Cabell wrote:

You must be surprised at the slow progress of our bill. The tardiness of its movement is to be regretted. But I do not know how it could be avoided. If it had been called up out of its regular turn, perhaps the irregularity of the course might give rise to animadversions. It will be read, in its turn, for the first time, today or tomorrow. It went through the committee without opposition. It will doubtless be opposed in the House, but from everything I can learn I think there cannot be much doubt of its success. . . .[18]

And Cabell was right, for within a few weeks the bill was law and one financial obstacle had been cleared. The troubles with the legislature were not over, to be sure, but on March 7, 1825, the university opened. One of Jefferson's four educational objectives had at long last been realized.

It is difficult to evaluate Jefferson's influence on higher education. Granted that the elective system originated in the University of Virginia and can be traced back to his writings, it was a long time before the system became widely adopted in the United States.

And in recent years there has been a tendency to regard the whole development as a tragedy (a view, by the way, which I do not hold). The University of Virginia was a state-supported university, but not the first; this honor is usually accorded to the University of North Carolina, which was chartered by the state legislature on December 11, 1789, and opened its doors in 1795. The University of Georgia had been chartered still earlier but did not open until 1801. By 1825, when the University of Virginia opened its doors, nine public institutions had been founded as universities. The University of Virginia, however, in the period 1825 to 1860 was one of the few which endeavored with some success to be a university in the European sense of that word. Furthermore, it set the tone for other universities. "This institution will be based on the illimitable freedom of the human mind," wrote Jefferson in 1820. "For here we are not afraid to follow truth wherever it may lead, nor to tolerate any error so long as reason is free to combat it." [19] Not only was the University of Virginia's influence throughout the South enormous in these years, but the example of what a publicly financed and publicly managed institution could accomplish must have affected policy in many of the newer states which were rapidly being admitted to the Union. One could almost say that the shape of higher education in the West before the Morrill Act [20] was largely fashioned in Virginia. It would be fame enough for anybody except Thomas Jefferson to have played so significant a part in the development of one phase of American education.

From the point of view of one interested in the history of American public education, Jefferson's failures are quite as interesting as his triumphs. At all events, I hope I may devote the remainder of this chapter to this topic without being accused of trying to dim the reputation of an educational statesman, clearly one of the most original in the history of the world. Let me turn to Jefferson's life-long efforts on behalf of providing free elementary education for all. The Virginia legislature in 1796 had passed a bill that purported to provide such education, but it was a fraud, for, as Jefferson wrote in his autobiography:

And in the Elementary bill, they inserted a provision which completely defeated it; for they left it to the court of each county to determine for itself, when this act should be carried into execution, within their county. One provision of the bill was, that the expenses of these schools should be borne by the inhabitants of the county, every one in proportion to his general tax rate. This would throw on wealth the education of the poor; and the justices, being generally of the more wealthy class, were unwilling to incur that burden, and I believe it was not suffered to commence in a single county.[21]

The bill passed by the Virginia legislature on February 21, 1818, twenty-two years later, might be considered a step in the direction of making elementary education free but hardly a step in making education free *for all*. It appropriated $45,000 annually from a special state fund—the Literary Fund—for the education of *poor* children. No provision was made for free education for the others. Honeywell (p. 21) writes of this outcome as follows:

The enactment of this law can be said to be a triumph for Jefferson's plan for primary schools only in the particular that it took from the courts the discretion left them by the law of 1796 [which had resulted in the law's being thwarted]. His friends accepted a system of schools for the poor in which they did not believe in order to get the University established. He always believed it to be inefficient and wasteful and more than once urged an attempt to remedy its defects.

But, since I have read W. A. Maddox's analysis of the action of the Virginia legislature in the sessions of 1816–1817 and 1817–1818, this statement of Honeywell's seems to me unsatisfactory. Neither at this point nor elsewhere in his exhaustive discussion of Jefferson's efforts on behalf of education does Honeywell expose clearly the clash of political forces which so profoundly influenced the educational history of Virginia in these two critical winters. I find Maddox's verdict justified by the evidence I have seen. He writes, "Jefferson's insistence on an extreme decentralized school policy must have retarded primary school legislation and development in the early nineteenth century quite as much as his philosophy of education in a democracy may have stimulated the rising spirit of Jacksonianism in the West." [22]

It is an historical fact that a bill providing for a system of public schools, sponsored by Charles Fenton Mercer, passed the Virginia House of Delegates in February, 1817, but was defeated in the Senate by a tie vote of 7-7.[23] Cabell endeavored to amend the bill before the final vote by requiring that the site of the proposed University of Virginia be Charlottesville.[24] Having failed in this endeavor he seems to have lent his influence (and indirectly therefore that of Jefferson's) to a defeat of the proposal.

It is difficult to assess all the reasons which led Jefferson to oppose Mercer's bill, but a comparison of his own drafts of legislation of 1817 with the Mercer bill as it passed the House of Delegates [25] brings out the following divergencies. First and foremost, Mercer was in favor of placing a great deal of power in what we would call today a state board of education. (And he vigorously defended this position in an address at Princeton ten years later.) Second, he proposed to use the income from the state "Literary Fund" for an entire system of public schools *with the first charge being for the purpose of the primary schools.* Third, even at the primary level of schooling, the board of trustees of each school was empowered to charge fees to "such parents, guardians or masters as are able to pay without inconvenience." Except for these three rather significant points Mercer's bill aimed to accomplish much of what Jefferson had proposed in 1779 and in a modified form had again proposed in 1817. Jefferson's selective principle (as I have ventured to call it) is incorporated in Mercer's proposed legislation. For in Sect. III the state board of public instruction is authorized

to provide some just and practical mode of advancing, from the primary schools to the academies, from the academies to the college [there were to be several of them], and from these to the university, *as many of the most meritorious children of indigence, as the revenue of the literary fund may suffice to educate and maintain* [italics mine], after the whole system of public instruction, which the board may devise, shall have been put in operation. In framing this system, the board shall regard the primary schools as its foundation . . .

A fundamental difference in political philosophy certainly separated Mercer and his supporters from Jefferson and his friends. In his writings at this time as well as before and after, Jefferson expressed both fear and scorn when contemplating a centralized state authority in education. Mercer was a Federalist and did not share the Jeffersonian views about the dangers of either the federal or state governments becoming too powerful. Perhaps the opposition between the views as to the political structure of a public school system was irreconcilable and sufficient to explain Jefferson's position. Yet as I have pointed out earlier, Jefferson was by no means consistent in his writings about the role of the state in education.

The second difference I have noted was essentially a practical one. Repeatedly in his correspondence with Cabell, Jefferson took the position that the Literary Fund was sufficient only for one purpose, namely, establishing a university. It was out of the question to assume that it was or would become large enough to support even in part an entire school system founded on primary schools. And to me this objection seems quite valid. The experience of other states showed that, unless there had been some financial miracle in Virginia, the elementary schools might have hobbled along with state aid but there would have been no state university.[26] The third divergence between Mercer and Jefferson in 1817 is one which the passage of time altered, strangely enough not because they came to share the same opinion but because each reversed his judgment, and the point at issue assumed more and more importance as public schools continued to multiply throughout the United States.

In 1817, Jefferson is on record as demanding that the elementary schools, at least for three years, be free for rich and poor alike. Mercer was willing to have the local trustees charge tuition fees to those families that could afford it. By 1820, when the subject of elementary education was once again up for discussion in Virginia, Jefferson was writing to Cabell that "those of them [the inhabitants of the ward] who are able, paying for the tuition of their own children, would leave no call on the public fund, but for the tuition fee of here and there an incidental pauper who would still be fed and lodged with his parents." [27] Thus, in his old age in his search for some way of establishing primary schools with little cost, Jefferson abandoned the first of the four objectives of his original proposals of 1779.

At about this time Mercer (now a member of Congress) appears to have changed his mind. For in the Princeton address of 1826 to which I have already referred, Mercer came out quite strongly for the "total abolition, in the elementary schools, of the odious distinction between the children of the opulent and of the poor." "A discrimination in the same schools, between the children of different parents . . . ," he declares, "should be avoided as alike incompatible with future harmony and happiness of both." [28]

What actually happened in Virginia as a result of the clash of opinions in the legislatures of 1817 and 1818 was a complete failure to establish public elementary schools on any principle. Indeed, it is a bit ironical to find that the University of Virginia was authorized by what amounted to a rider on a bill providing for the distribution of state funds for the education of the children of the poor. For the law starts by establishing school commissioners, who were to select "so many poor children as they may deem expedient" and send them "to such school as may be convenient to be taught reading, writing and arithmetic." These provisions were totally unlike those Jefferson had proposed in 1779 or in his bill of 1817–1818.

In the letter of November, 1820, to Cabell, in which he appears to retreat from his advocacy of elementary schools *free for all*, he compares education in New York with that in Virginia, very much to the disadvantage of his native state. "Six thousand common schools in New York, fifty pupils each, 300,000 in all; $160,000 annually paid to the masters. . . . What a pygmy to this is Virginia become!" he declares, and, raising the question, "Whence this difference?" answers by the flat statement, "From the difference their rulers set on the value of knowledge and the prosperity it produces." [29] Yet the revenues to pay for the elementary schools in the state Jefferson so much admired were to a large extent raised by charging a tuition fee to all but the indigent families. And this rate-bill system continued for fifty years and was only abolished after a long struggle. To be sure, New York state had early appropriated state funds to encourage local communities to establish public schools. The Act of 1795 had gone so far as to require each town to raise half as much more by tax as it received from the state. But those who framed the act had no idea that *all* the funds required for public schools would be raised by state or local taxes. They assumed, as did many of their contemporaries, that much of the money would come from tuition fees. In other words, they started from the premise that "primarily the responsibility rested upon each individual to educate his offspring, and that only when he failed to do this, private or public charity might properly aid the unfortunate." [30] The New York system in the first half of the nineteenth century, in short, was a system by which taxes only helped to support publicly managed elementary schools, which charged tuition fees.

The way the rate bill was used in the state of New York was described in an official document in 1848 as follows:

The trustees [the local board] employ a qualified teacher for stipulated wages. At the close of his term, they give him an order upon

33

the town superintendent for such portion of the public money, as may have been voted by the district. . . . If the public money is not sufficient to pay the teacher's wages, the trustees proceed to make out a rate-bill for the residue, charging each parent or guardian, according to the number of days' attendance of his children. Under the present law, the trustees have power to exempt indigent persons, and the amount exempted is a charge upon the district, and may be immediately collected by tax, or added to any tax thereafter levied.

As the state superintendent went on to say,

A more troublesome or vexatious system could not well be devised. . . . The rate-bill system requires every person to pay in proportion to the attendance of his children. . . . How strong then is the inducement of many parents to wink at absence and truancy. . . '. The fact that the number of children attending school less than four months, uniformly exceeds the number attending a longer time furnishes strong evidence for believing that the rate-bill system is the principal cause of irregular attendance of scholars.[31]

The report from which I have just quoted was in essence a plea to the legislature to establish a system of really free elementary schools. To the taxpayer's objections—and they were vigorous—the writer appealed to the self-interest of property owners. The Superintendent of Common Schools, the author of the report, pointed out that "property is the creature of law" and "the security of property is one of the paramount objects of government." He then asks the question, "How shall that security be attained? By the stern restraints and crushing force of military power?" And answers these questions by referring to the revolutions in Europe of that year (1848), and contrasting the "uncertainty and insecurity . . . stamped upon all things" on that continent with "a change in the policy of the government" of the United States brought about by a presidential election accomplished "with the cheerful and peaceful acquiescence of the Union." From which the proponent of free schools draws the conclusion that, "There is a moral and intellectual power in the universal education of the people which furnishes more abiding security for persons and property than disciplined armies. Property must be taxed to support soldiery. Why should it not then contribute to a system of protection which may preclude the necessity of armies?"[32] A similar argument we

34

find repeated in more than one state in this period of American history. The urbanization of the nation had begun and with it had arisen the problem of law and order among the impoverished city dwellers, who often were ready to resort to violent demonstrations which frightened the well-to-do.

It was the voters of the cities, not the rural and town taxpayers, who eventually succeeded in abolishing the rate-bill system. The New York legislature of 1849 passed an "act establishing free schools throughout the state," which was referred to the voters on a state-wide referendum. The vote was 249,872 in favor and 91,951 against. But four important rural counties returned majorities against the bill. That is, they wanted to retain the rate-bill system. When one considers that at that time and for some years before something like 40 per cent of the resources of the schools came from the rates charged parents, one sees why the taxpayers who were not parents were in revolt. Indeed, it proved so difficult to transfer at once this financial load onto the counties and local communities that it became impossible to put the new law into effect. A petition for repeal resulted in another state-wide referendum, and though repeal was defeated the margin was small. Only the voters in the cities carried the day.[33] The Superintendent of Public Instruction of New York forty years later described what happened next as follows:

In 1850, a kind of compromise was effected, and the controversy was attempted to be settled by restoring the rate-bill and levying a state tax for $800,000, to be distributed with the school money. . . . But as a general thing the cities would not tolerate the rate-bill. At their solicitation the Legislature, from time to time, passed special acts creating a board of education with general powers and duties, and in this manner set up an organized school system in each city. These special laws ordinarily authorized taxation adequate to the entire support of the schools, and thus the rate-bill became obsolete in most of the cities at a comparatively early day. . . . In 1867 . . . the rate-bill system was finally abolished and the principle that the schools should be absolutely free to all and supported at public and general expense, was fully and triumphantly established.[34]

What had been going on in New York City during the same period is of interest as showing the variety of ways free education for the poor might be provided.[35] A private organization chartered by the state managed free elementary schools in that city for nearly fifty years "for the education of such poor children as do not belong to or are not provided for by any religious society." As late as 1841, the schools of this society, known as the Public School Society, and schools of various churches were the only free schools in the city. At that time, the State Superintendent of Common Schools estimated that less than half the children in the city between four and sixteen were receiving the benefit of education.[36] A year later the legislature established a Board of Education in New York City with authority to set up free public schools in each ward. For over a decade, two systems of free schools existed side by side in New York City. The Public School Society received funds from year to year by grants from the Board of Education. The growing numbers attending the schools managed by the Board of Education and the financial difficulties of the Public School Society led to a peaceful merger of the two competing systems in 1853.[37] One pattern of free schools—a system of publicly subsidized private schools—was thus abandoned. The merger came just at the time the cities had registered their objection to the rate-bill system. I think it fair to say that public opinion in New York City had been shown to be strongly against two methods of financing and managing free schools and had settled on what we now regard as the characteristic American pattern.

Yet it is worth noting that in New York state the pressure for establishing what has become a characteristic of our system did not come from the families long settled in that part of the United States. Quite the contrary. It came from the immigrants who crowded in the cities. They were without property to be taxed, but many of them had a vote, and they demanded education. The continuing struggle between the taxpayer and the educator which characterizes all periods of our history finally resulted in New York state in the acceptance of what I have called Jefferson's first objective: free elementary schools for all. All the other states which had used the rate-bill system had abandoned it by 1871.

There is little evidence to indicate that in New York or in any other state the memory of Jefferson's eloquent arguments played an important part. To be sure, Stephen Simpson dedicated a little volume entitled *A Manual for Workingmen* to the shade of Jefferson. The volume, published in 1831, contained a strong plea for a "system of popular education" and speaks of the "odious system of charity schools" ordained by the "rich who have heretofore been our sole law makers." [38] Similar arguments by workingmen's associations might be considered a continuation of the Jeffersonian tradition on behalf of free education for all. But in general one hunts in vain to find references to Jefferson in the writings of the proponents of public schools in the period 1830 to 1860. Jefferson's reputation was in eclipse.[39] Virginia had made no progress in developing free schools. Those who were proponents of universal education had to look elsewhere for a model, to what was happening in New England in the 1830's and 1840's. They also looked, strangely enough, overseas to Prussia.[40]

A French professor of philosophy, Victor Cousin, had made a trip to Germany in 1831 and reported what he saw to the French government. His report was translated into English and republished in New York in 1835.[41] In general, his comments on Prussian education were highly favorable, particularly on the training of teachers. Calvin E. Stowe, an American professor, also reported favorably on Prussian education to the legislature of the state of Ohio at about the same time. His report was printed and widely circulated.[42] (A decade later his wife, Harriet Beecher Stowe, published her *Uncle Tom's Cabin* with even greater success!) From Europe came evidence of what a state with state funds could accomplish by establishing a complete system of education.

To be sure, the Prussian kings had not been the first to establish compulsory elementary education. Long before Frederick William I, the Puritan founders of the Massachusetts Bay Colony had produced the same results, but for very different reasons. The laws of 1645 and 1647 passed by the General Court of the Bay Colony are often referred to as the basis of our present system of local control. How much validity there is in this statement, is a question I shall return to shortly. The Puritans wanted compulsory education for the same reason that John Knox wanted it—to perpetuate a theocracy. The Prussians wanted it in order to have a well-ordered monarchy. Jefferson had wanted it to render the "people the safe guardians of their liberties." Conservatives in many states in the 1830's and 1840's were coming to favor it because of their fear of an unruly urban proletariat and the power of demagogues over an illiterate mass of voters.

The Prussian example was on the side of state-directed schools. New England precedent was on the side of local schools. The taxpayer was in general opposed to free schools at his expense. And in those days local taxes were the issue. In general the state had no source of revenue except local taxes, and in this period of history no one was interested in building up the power of the state government by enlarging the purse at its disposal.[43] Yet something had to be done. This was evident to a man like Edmund Dwight, a graduate of Yale in the class of 1799, who made a large fortune developing the textile industry along the Connecticut River in Massachusetts. By 1841 his mills employed 3,000 people, a large number for those days. His success had literally created one-industry towns which later became cities. His biographer writes, "Less spectacular than his business ventures was his notable contribution to the development of public education." [44] This started by his reading Victor Cousin's report on education in Prussia and continued by his being one of a group who persuaded the Massachusetts legislature to pass a law in 1837 setting up the State Board of Education, of which he became a member, and arranging for the appointment of Horace Mann as secretary. Finally he gave the state anonymously a sum of money which enabled Mann to open the first state normal school in Lexington, Massachusetts, in 1839.[45]

In spite of having read about Prussian education, Dwight had no idea of copying the state system, even without the monarch. The Massachusetts law of 1837 provided only for a State Board of Education with a secretary who was to collect information from the cities and towns in regard to education. Mann did two things of great importance which have assured him a place of high honor among American educators, though he served only twelve years as Secretary of the Massachusetts Board of Education. He toured the state, collected information, and more or less shamed the localities into putting their local schools in order. He concerned himself with the appointment of teachers and, stimulated no doubt by the writings of a Massachusetts schoolmaster (James G. Carter) who served in the legislature, he established the first state school for training teachers.[46] At just about this time Henry Barnard, like Mann trained as a lawyer and active in politics, became interested in improving education in Connecticut. Both Mann and Barnard, through their writings, had an enormous effect on the thinking of Americans about education at the period when the problems became acute. Both stood firmly for local schools, locally managed and largely locally financed. One can hardly doubt that their influence played an important part in the final victory of the friends of free public schools in New York state in the 1850's and 1860's. By the 1870's, the present pattern of local control and local financing of elementary schools was established in many, if not all, states of the Union.[47] Such schools became known as common schools, since they were common to all, rich and poor alike.

It was no accident that the push for educational reform came from New England.

The entire period (1820–1850) is characterized by the rapid growth of urban population, the development of manufacture and a multiplicity of important inventions. The population of Massachusetts increased during the two decades, 1800–1820, nearly 24 percent; during 1820–1840, over 40 percent; during 1830–1850, nearly 60 percent; but during the same periods the increase in the population of the City of Boston was approximately 73, 115, and 123 percent respectively. Lowell, which had no existence in 1820, boasted of a population of over 20,000 in 1840. . . . In the three New England States of Massachusetts, Rhode Island, and Connecticut during the period from 1820–1840, the number of persons engaged in agriculture increased approximately one-fourth; those engaged in commerce decreased about one-third; and those engaged in manufacture and trades increased nearly two and one-half times.[48]

And it was no accident that the first push for educational reform came in Massachusetts. But one is tempted to say that it was an historical accident that vigorous industrialization and its attendant urbanization should have started, thanks in part to abundant water power, in exactly that portion of the North American continent where two centuries earlier a Puritan theocracy had established local schools and attempted to enforce compulsory school attendance. The theocracy had long since vanished. The state laws requiring the towns to maintain free schools were largely honored in the breach at the time the process of industrialization began. But the tradition persisted of proudly independent communities supporting and managing their own schools by general taxation. No rate-bill system had been introduced; no state tax to support schools had been even contemplated. The contrast with New York is clear. Horace Mann grasped the significance of the old Puritan tradition, strengthened it, and proclaimed it widely throughout the nation. It became the pattern of American public education. Jefferson's first objective—the establishment of schools publicly managed and free for all—which he seemed to have forsaken in his old age, thus became the accepted American doctrine fifty years after he was dead. It became so in part thanks to his own political activity, for the spread of universal male suffrage had proved to be a potent force. But, ironically enough, this force gained its predominant strength from the very developments Jefferson as a young man had dreaded most—industrialization and urbanization.[49] So little can reformers foresee the nature of their future allies!

3

The Relevance of
Jefferson's Ideas Today

I N THE FIRST CHAPTER, I considered Thomas
Jefferson as an educational innovator. In the second, I considered his success in establishing the University of Virginia
and his failure to persuade the legislature of his state to
establish a system of free public elementary schools. In connection
with this failure, I traced the slow development of a concept we
now take for granted, namely, that public schools should be free
for children of the rich and poor alike, that they should be locally
managed and largely locally financed as well. As I pointed out, only
the social forces generated by industrialization and urbanization
finally led about the year 1870 to the establishment of what might
be called the characteristic American pattern of common schools.

The doctrine which became widely accepted by the 1870's applied, however, only to elementary schools. The struggle to extend
free education upwards, so to speak, to lengthen the course eventually to include twelve grades, at least for some—this struggle occurred between 1870 and 1890. I must now devote some pages to it
because the history of secondary education bears directly on the
subject of this chapter: the relevance of Jefferson's ideas for us
today. For it is only the selective features of Jefferson's proposals—

his second and third objectives, as I have called them—that seem to have relevance for our current discussion of American education. We take for granted our public elementary schools, free for rich and poor alike and largely locally financed, as Jefferson advocated for many years. Likewise we accept without a moment's hesitation Jefferson's arguments in favor of a state university. Many of his wonderful phrases about education and the government of a free people seem as applicable to the United States in the 1960's as they were, in his eyes, to the young republic of the late eighteenth century. One might be inclined to say that his basic ideas about elementary education, on the one hand, and university education, on the other, are so relevant as to be commonplace. However, when we consider what he wrote in 1781 or later in 1814 and 1818 about secondary education, awkward questions soon arise. Many of his assumptions seem out of date.

When we examine details, we become aware of the fact that we are living in an educational world of which Jefferson could never have dreamed. Our free public secondary schools in many states now accommodate a majority of the youth between 14 and 18; in some states 80 per cent of an age group complete twelve years of elementary and secondary schooling. State universities and colleges in several states provide instruction for all high school graduates either without charge or for a relatively low fee. Scholarships to private institutions of higher education are available on what to Jefferson would have seemed an impossibly lavish scale. His selective principle, he might say, has become a vast scheme of college scholarships. But another method of providing college and university education for the poor boy had slowly developed throughout the nineteenth and early twentieth centuries which made scholarships seem unnecessary. The American tradition of working one's way through college had become an established practice and to many Americans seemed more democratic than receiving financial aid, which smacked of charity distributed to the poor. By 1960, a revived interest in scholarships together with the opportunities of earning money while going to college enabled a host of young people to receive higher education with little or no cost to their families.

Have all these developments rendered obsolete Jefferson's concern with the education of the "best geniuses"? Have we long since reached a point where in every state, the state avails itself "of those talents which nature has sown as liberally among the poor as the rich, but which perish without use"? In short, can we say we have a uniform educational policy throughout the nation which meets the twentieth-century equivalent of the needs Jefferson had in mind when he spoke of his total plan as the "keystone of the arch of our government"? Are "worth and genius" today sought out "from every condition of life" and "carefully prepared by education" for "public trusts"? These are some of the questions I propose to examine after reviewing briefly the genesis of our present public secondary school system.

As a guide to the somewhat complex history of public education during the last hundred years, I offer three hypotheses:

First, our educational history is bound up with the reluctance of the taxpayer to pay taxes. Second, over the years this reluctance has taken somewhat different forms and has been overcome in different ways. From 1800 to 1870, for example, the taxpayer objected to paying even for elementary schooling for all except the children of the very poor. Later the development of the high school ran into financial difficulties. Third, only in the 1950's did the national picture so alter that Jefferson's selective principle, viewed as a nation-wide scholarship policy, seemed to have relevance for the United States and therefore became part of our thinking about education.

Armed with these three hypotheses, I will examine the far from simple story of the evolution of our pattern of education. The American public high school did not come into being overnight. Quite the contrary. The present institution is the result of a long process of evolution. (Some of the bitter critics of American public schools would undoubtedly say a long process of devolution!) In Jefferson's youth, the grammar school was the widely accepted type of secondary school. As he outlined in his first comprehensive plan, the youth in these schools were to become proficient in the use of those intellectual tools which were then essential for learned men. I refer, of course, to a mastery of Latin and Greek (to these, by the way, Jefferson added French as equally essential). These grammar schools had flourished up and down the Atlantic Coast in colonial times. In New England some of these schools could claim an ancestry going back to the middle of the seventeenth century. Many were publicly managed and publicly supported. Rival institutions known as "academies" began to appear in the second half of the eighteenth century, and rapidly increased in numbers and popularity after the American Revolution.[1] Many served local communities. Others, like the Phillips Academies of Exeter, New Hampshire, and Andover, Massachusetts, were in part boarding schools and came to serve a national clientele. Though nowadays those endowed academies, which can boast of an eighteenth-century heritage, are primarily college preparatory boarding schools, they were not so in origin. Rather they were established as alternatives to the grammar schools, which were concerned with preparing boys to enter the few universities (actually colleges) which then existed. The academies were expressly established to give practical instruction for those not preparing for college. Academies were private institutions chartered by the state, largely depending on endowment and tuition fees. The possibility of receiving public support was by no means excluded; by the second quarter of the nineteenth century a number of academies in various states were the recipients of state funds.[2]

The rivalry between the new private academies and the older local public schools, which was to characterize the first fifty years of the nineteenth century, was foreseen by Samuel Adams in his inaugural address as Governor of Massachusetts in 1795. He commented:

It is with satisfaction that I have observed the patriotic exertions of worthy citizens to establish academies in various parts of the Commonwealth. It discovers a zeal highly to be commended. But while it is acknowledged that great advantages have been derived from these institutions, perhaps it may be justly apprehended that multiplying them may have a tendency to injure the ancient and beneficial mode of education in town grammar schools. The peculiar advantage of such schools is that the poor and the rich may derive equal benefit from them; but none excepting the more wealthy, generally speaking, can avail themselves of the benefits of the academies. Should these institutions detach the attention and influence of the wealthy from the generous support of the town schools, is it not to be feared that useful learning, instruction, and social feelings in the early parts of life may cease to be so equally and universally disseminated as it has heretofore been? [3]

What Governor Adams had feared actually came to pass to a large degree in his own state. By the middle of the nineteenth century the private academies had largely replaced the public grammar schools as the accepted type of institution to which the prosperous sent their children. To be sure, the academies usually offered the same instruction as did the old grammar schools, but they also offered some new courses, such as English.[4] The growing dissatisfaction of the prosperous merchant class with a purely classical education first found its expression in the curriculum of many of these academies. The middle class of Americans in the first decades of the nineteenth century were by no means as convinced as had been Jefferson that a young man needed to master two or three languages before he could serve the state. Eventually, older colleges like William and Mary, Harvard, Yale, Princeton, and Brown were forced to modify their courses of instruction, but the movement away from a strictly classical curriculum seems to have started in the private academies.

In the previous chapter, attention was drawn to the fact that the first push for educational reform came in Massachusetts—a consequence, I believe, of its early industrialization and urbanization. It is not surprising that a new type of public secondary school seems to have originated in that state in the 1820's. Josiah Quincy, the mayor of Boston, described the event shortly after it occurred in the following words: "In 1820, an English classical school was established, having for its object to enable the mercantile and mechanical classes to obtain an education adapted for those children whom their parents wished to qualify for active life, and thus relieve them from the necessity of incurring the expense incident to private academies." [5]

Eventually the competition between the new type of free public school (it was designated as the Boston English High School in 1824) and the private academies was to end with the disappearance of many of the latter. But for a generation or two most of the relatively few young men who obtained a full secondary education attended private academies. The public high school did not become popular until after the Civil War. In the 1830's there were well over 500 academies in sixteen Eastern states and not more than a dozen public high schools; twenty-five years later the number of high schools had only doubled.[6] This was the period when the rate-bill system discussed in the last chapter was in effect in New York and a number of other states. The reluctance of the taxpayer to provide free education for the children of those who could afford to pay now asserted itself at the secondary level.

Arguments went back and forth as to the relative merits of

private and public schools. George S. Boutwell, Governor of Massachusetts (1851–1855) and later Secretary of the Massachusetts Board of Education, was, like his predecessor Horace Mann, a strong proponent of public schools. Two of his lectures delivered in the late 1850's make interesting reading. "It is easy to enumerate the advantages of a system of public education, and the evils—I say evils —of endowed academies, whether free or charging payment for tuition," he declared. However, he did then go on to concede that "Endowed academies are not, in all respects, under all circumstances, and everywhere to be condemned." [7]

One argument which Boutwell advanced in regard to the merits of public secondary education would strike most of us as curious today, to say the least. He declared:

In the public high school we avoid a difficulty that is almost universal in academies and private schools—the presence of pupils whose attainments are so various that by a proper classification they would be assigned to two, if not to three grades, where the graded system exists. The vigilance, industry and fidelity of teachers cannot overcome this evil. The instruction given is inevitably less systematic and thorough. . . . There is also an inherent power of discipline in the public schools, where they are graded, and a system of examination exists, that is not found elsewhere. Neither the pupil nor the parent is viewed by the teacher in the light of a patron; hence he seeks only to so conduct his school as to meet the public requirement.[8]

Boutwell then goes on to imply that private academies have to admit students often because of family considerations, whereas the public schools admit on the basis of merit alone. And in this connection he stresses "the importance of a fixed standard of admission and a careful examination of the candidates." [9] This quotation serves to emphasize that originally and for many years the public high school was a selective institution, a fact that is often forgotten today.

In the standard textbooks on the history of American education, the Kalamazoo case is usually given much attention. That decision of the Supreme Court of the state of Michigan is generally regarded as marking the turning point in the development of the public high school. Without a great deal more statistical evidence covering many states, I should not wish to subscribe to what may be an oversimplification of history. How much the decision of one state supreme court influenced legal and educational opinion in other states is hard to say. But the case is of interest because it illustrates the point I have made so often, namely, the reluctance of the taxpayer to support new advances in public education.

In essence the case was as follows: A group of taxpayers in Kalamazoo, Michigan, had brought a bill of complaint before a lower state court to enjoin the collection of taxes for the support of a high school. The lower court dismissed the bill and the case was appealed to the state Supreme Court, which decided that the decree of the lower court was right and should be affirmed. The opinion of Justice Thomas M. Cooley, which was concurred in by all the other members of the court, is of so much interest that I venture to present it in abbreviated form in the following paragraphs.

"The bill in this case is filed to restrain the collection of such portion of the school taxes assessed against complainants for the year 1872, as have been voted for the support of the high school in that village," says Justice Cooley in the opening sentence of his opinion. He goes on to say:

. . . the real purpose of the suit is wider and vastly more comprehensive than this brief statement would indicate, inasmuch as it seeks a judicial determination of the right of school authorities, in what are called union school districts of the state, to levy taxes upon the general public for the support of what in this state are known as high schools, and to make free by such taxation the instruction of children in other languages than the English. The bill is consequently of no small interest to all the people of the state; and to a large number of very flourishing schools, it is of the very highest interest, as their prosperity and usefulness, in a large degree, depend upon the method in which they are supported, so that a blow at this method seems a blow at the schools themselves. . . . The complainants rely upon two objections to the taxes in question, one of which is general, and the other applies only to the authority or action of this particular district. . . . The more general question which the record presents we shall endeavor to state in our own language. . . . It is, as we understand it, that there is no authority in this state to make the high schools free by taxation levied on the people at large. . . . When this doctrine was broached to us, we must confess to no little surprise that the legislation and policy of our state were appealed to against the right of the state to furnish a liberal education to the youth of the state in schools brought within the reach of all classes.

. . . As this, however, is now so seriously disputed, it may be necessary, perhaps, to take a brief survey of the legislation and general course, not only of the state, but of the antecedent territory. . . .

The justice then summarized the territorial laws, including an Act of 1827, which he said was

a general law, which, under the name of common schools, required not only schools for elementary instruction, but also grammar schools to be maintained. The qualifications required in teachers of grammar schools were such as to leave it open to no doubt that grammar schools in the sense understood in England and the Eastern States were intended in which instruction in the classics should be given, as well as in such higher branches of learning as would not usually be taught in the schools of lowest grade.

"Thus stood the law," continued the justice, "when the constitution of 1835 was adopted." After quoting the sections of the constitution dealing with education, Justice Cooley concluded that no restriction was imposed upon the legislature as to the establishment of schools intermediate between the common schools (specified in the constitution) and the university specifically mentioned. Turning to the official report of the State Superintendent for 1837, he noted that the state official stated that the great object of common schools was "to furnish good instruction in all elementary and common branches of knowledge for all classes of the community, as good, indeed, for the poorest boy of the state as the rich man can furnish for his children with all his wealth." The context shows, the justice concludes, that the superintendent "had the systems of Prussia and of New England in view, and that he proposed by a free school system to fit the children of the poor as well as of the rich for the highest spheres of activity and influence."

Examining then the state constitution of 1850 and the discussion concerning schools in the state convention which framed this document, Justice Cooley draws the conclusion that "the people expected the tendency towards the establishment of high schools in the primary school districts would continue until every locality capable of supporting one was supplied." The concluding sentence of the opinion is:

We content ourselves with the statement that neither in our state policy, in our constitution, or in our laws, do we find the primary school districts restricted in the branches of knowledge which their officers may cause to be taught, or the grade of instruction that may be given, if their voters consent in regular form to bear the expense and raise the taxes for the purpose.[10]

Whether or not the Kalamazoo case had the effect on the national scene usually attributed to it, there can be no doubt that in the 1870's and 1880's, the number of public high schools increased rapidly and by 1890 public schools were enrolling 69 per cent of secondary school students the country over. By 1900, the figure had increased to 82 per cent. Publicly managed local schools, tax-supported, free to all, had become the characteristic feature of American secondary education. In at least two states the public high schools by the end of the century were tied more closely to a university than the old grammar schools had ever been. A so-called accrediting system was introduced in the state of Michigan in 1871. Through a purely voluntary agreement between the state university and the schools, the university provided for an annual inspection of each high school by a committee of faculty members. A few years later a similar scheme was introduced in California and in a much modified form continues to the present day.[11]

At the turn of the twentieth century, the public high school had become the recognized form of public secondary school. In those older states where the public grammar schools had once characterized the educational scene, the grammar schools had either disappeared or changed their names to Latin schools. Private secondary schools continued and were of special significance in the East where they served as preparatory schools for the Eastern colleges, which in some instances enrolled more than half of their freshmen classes from these schools. The differences between the public high school and the private college preparatory school sixty years ago was not very great in terms of program or academic standards. Indeed, instances could be cited where Boutwell's words of forty years earlier applied; some of the high schools may well have had higher academic standards than some private preparatory schools. The public high school, however, was about to undergo a profound modification.

Just how different the situation was in 1902 from what it became 15 or 20 years later is well illustrated by a quotation from the introductory chapter of an excellent book on *The Making of Our Mid-*

dle Schools by Elmer E. Brown, Professor of the Theory and Practice of Education in the University of California. Professor Brown wrote as follows:

Primary education . . . is the education needed for all; which for the sake of the general good, no citizen can be permitted to do without. Beyond this is the region of difference, of divergence, and it may be added, of very great uncertainty and dispute. Occasionally one hears the prophecy that what we call secondary education will eventually be an education for all. It is now the lower stage of the education that cannot be for all, and the stage in which differentiation according to the individual's prospective service to society, or according to the individual's peculiar tastes and capacities, or according to both of these together, finds its beginning. Secondary education is differentiated education in its earlier processes. It makes the preliminary survey of the students' special aptitudes and capacities, with a view to discovering to himself and to those interested in his future, what there is in him that may be made of most worth to society, and so most serviceable to his own self-realization.[12]

The statement I have quoted was written in 1902. One sentence stands out as summing up the status of public secondary education at that time and raised a vigorous question mark for the twentieth century that then lay ahead: "Occasionally one hears the prophecy that what we call secondary education will eventually be an education for all." And Professor Brown goes on to say, "It is now the lower stage of the education that cannot be for all."

I have no reliable figures as to the fraction of the youth in different states attending high school in 1900. It is safe to say that in no community was it large. As late as 1916, the Superintendent of Public Schools in Berkeley, California, was writing that "enrollment rapidly diminishes as one proceeds upward in the grades of our public schools. The eighth grade is always very much smaller than preceding ones, and frequently, in a given school, is only large enough to maintain one or two classes." [13] Such a shrinkage in the size of grade 8, by the way, was one of the chief arguments presented by the proponents of the junior high school.

At the beginning of the twentieth century in some states a poor but able and industrious student could receive a secondary education locally at public expense. In many but by no means all towns this education would have included a rather long study of orthodox

50

academic subjects. In Lowell High School of San Francisco, for example, in 1901 there were four courses or programs.[14] In all four, Latin was studied four or five times a week for two years, and mathematics and English for approximately the same length of time for four years. Greek was required in one program, French or German or both, in two of the others. Science was required, though not every day, every year, in all courses; it was more heavily emphasized in the program known as the scientific.

The programs offered in the Lowell High School in 1901 were not exceptional. In the high schools of many if not all the cities in the United States, it was then expected that college-bound students would study at least two foreign languages for a period of four years. The three possibilities open to the students in the San Francisco school remind me of the three types of Gymnasia now available in Germany and Switzerland for those who can qualify and who wish to head for a university. Indeed, I am tempted to write that the American public high schools at the start of this century were similar to the European system of pre-university schools which has continued to the present day. However, there are three important differences to be noted. And each is of importance for an understanding of what has happened in this country in this century. In the first place, in European countries the state has always determined the standards of admission to the pre-university schools and to the university. Even in a federated nation like Switzerland or Germany today, the standards are essentially the same throughout the nation. Second, the pre-university school—the Gymnasium or the French *lycée* or the English grammar school—prepares its graduates to enter into a university, *not* a college. The school includes the first two or three years of an American undergraduate college. Third, the programs offered in universities at the undergraduate level in the United States were by 1900 so wide in range as to include courses which were outside the scope of what had hitherto been known as academic subjects.

During the closing decades of the nineteenth century a disconcerting question had been often raised: Is the type of general education required of a future member of the learned professions necessarily the best type of general education for the future businessman or farmer? And America's heretical negative answer was already to be heard when the twentieth century began.

One must remember that the four-year undergraduate course

leading to a bachelor's degree is in the nature of an historical accident. What was believed in the first half of the nineteenth century to be the necessary preparation for university work had become entangled with the idea of the proper education for a gentleman. The process of untangling these ideas is still continuing. Yet even as late as 1850 there were no universities in the United States in the European or British sense of that word. Postgraduate study for law and medicine was essentially unknown before the 1880's. The preparation for these professions and that of engineering was commenced directly after the completion of a secondary school course. (I may note parenthetically that, by a curious twist of academic history, law and medical schools became essentially postgraduate by the end of the nineteenth century, while engineering schools did not; they retain their special position to the present day.) Advanced work in science and letters leading to a Ph.D. was hardly possible in the United States until D. C. Gilman in the 1870's in opening Johns Hopkins University started to domesticate the European university tradition. This was a revolutionary step. But even more revolutionary had been the establishment a few decades earlier of agricultural and mechanical arts colleges. The passage of the Morrill Act during the Civil War provided each state with federal funds in support of what came to be known as land-grant colleges.[15] The two revolutions were in one sense complementary to each other; in another sense they were contradictory or at least out of phase. The founding of Johns Hopkins University led to the development of graduate schools of arts and sciences in many universities and greatly strengthened the scholarly and scientific traditions of their faculties.[16] Status was given to advanced academic work as those words were understood in Europe. The growth of the land-grant colleges gave status to practical activities, originally agriculture and mechanics. As the nineteenth century drew to a close, these institutions more and more enlarged their offerings. They were prepared to grant a degree for the completion of a course of study in many fields which hitherto had not been regarded as lying within the province of a university, certainly not in Europe. The effect of this enlargement of the scope of the work suitable for candidates for a first degree had a pronounced effect on public secondary education. The effect has become more pronounced the last few decades because, in addition to the universities, many a so-called liberal arts college has become what might be called a widely comprehensive institution; [17] some, indeed, grant degrees to almost anyone who will remain in residence four years.

But let me return to history and the year 1900. The influence of the expanded function of public institutions of higher education was enormously reinforced during the next thirty years by the shift in the employment picture. In a lecture I gave at Harvard in 1959 I ventured to speak of the changes in this century as "The Revolutionary Transformation of the American High School"; I related this transformation to the altered status of youth in employment, and I raised the question whether this change was a reversible social process comparable to prohibition, or irreversible like the transformation of our habits of locomotion. I concluded that the process was irreversible, and challenged all who disagreed with me to try to obtain the repeal of the mass of state and federal laws which now govern the employment of youth.[18] And after they had done that, to persuade management and labor unions to alter their attitude toward the full-time employment of boys and girls 14, 15, and 16 years of age.

It is impossible to summarize all the historical evidence that leads me to my conclusion. I might note, however, that as late as 1910, 30 per cent of the youth 14 and 15 years of age were employed, while by 1930, the figure had dropped to 9 per cent. The school enrollment had correspondingly increased. As a secondary factor in the change, the depression of the 1930's played an important part. The experiment with part-time education provided in continuation schools (somewhat on the European plan) was abandoned. Vocational courses financed by federal funds, under the Smith-Hughes Act, began to flourish.[19]

The evidence is clear. We cannot turn the educational clock backwards; we could not, even if we wished, return to the situation of 1900 or even 1916. Some might be inclined to say that as a result of the radical shifts of the last fifty or sixty years, now everyone goes to college. Of course, this is far from being the case. In some communities, in some states, only half the age group graduates from high school; in others, to be sure, the figure is well over 80 per cent. From the point of view of the welfare of society, the question can be raised: Does the large fraction of the youth which in many states attends a college or university comprise essentially all who have academic talent? The country over, how many potential lawyers, doctors, engineers, scientists, and scholars are we failing to educate?

53

If Jefferson were alive today, these are the types of questions I am bold enough to think he might well ask.

The need for more and better scholarship provisions is an old hobby of mine. In pushing my arguments for more funds for scholarships in the bleak years of the depression I often invoked the memory of Jefferson and quoted those famous phrases with which he justified his selective scheme for the education of the poor boy.[20] Over the past twenty-five years, I must admit I have frequently encountered something less than enthusiasm for my plea for a renewal of Jefferson's concern with "raking the geniuses from the rubbish." (I was never so tactless as to quote these particular words, of course.) I soon found that, whatever words one used, preferential treatment of one group of youths over another, which is implicit in all scholarship proposals, goes against the grain of many educators. Selection means competition, and for many years school people have tended to frown on competition. I sympathize with the origin of this prejudice—a reaction against some of the European practices which tend to substitute an academic contest for the development of a love of learning. But like all reactions, this one went too far in the 1930's. It was not only certain educators, however, who were indifferent or hostile to the Jeffersonian selective tradition. Laymen, especially taxpayers, were hostile, too. Let me recount only one episode to illustrate my point that by 1945 "equality of opportunity" meant for most Americans the same number of years of free education for everyone. And since prestige and length of formal exposure to teaching had become so closely associated, equality of status under those circumstances was brought in complete harmony with equality of opportunity.

The incident I have in mind involved the action of a committee of the House of Representatives of the 78th Congress of the United States. To this committee had been referred in the late fall of 1943 a message from President Roosevelt, transmitting a "Preliminary Report of the Armed Forces Committee on Post-War Educational Opportunities for Service Personnel." What was at issue was the nature of what became known as the educational provisions of the G.I. Bill of Rights. The committee, among other recommendations, included one that read as follows:

. . . the Committee believes it should be made financially possible for a limited number of exceptionally able ex-service personnel to carry on their education for a period of 1, 2, and in some instances as much as 3 additional years, provided:

1. That completion of the courses they are taking will serve to meet recognized needs;

2. That by superior performance on a *competitive basis* they have demonstrated the likelihood that they will profit from these courses; and

3. That they continue to make satisfactory progress in the courses and to give promise of future usefulness.[21] [Italics mine.—J. B. C.]

The proposed financial provisions were generous. The whole scheme, I submit, might be regarded as a 1943 version of Jefferson's selective ideas for secondary and university education with the exception that the benefits were to accrue to the rich and poor alike. As I recall the discussions, the possibility of requiring proof of financial need was considered and decisively rejected.

I had had no part in preparing the proposals which were before Congress. I found myself, however, drawn into the discussions. Or perhaps it would be more accurate to state that I undertook to do a little lobbying. I had no luck at all. One officer representing the War Department was more than cool to the idea of using public funds for education on a competitive basis. To my arguments that there was a shortage of able men with professional postgraduate training, he suggested that those who wanted years of study in a university should pay for it themselves, and added that, instead of spending more money on the brightest boy, as I suggested, if anything we should provide the *others* with more education because they needed it the most! "At all events, we have never had in the United States," he said, "any such doctrine as you suggest and we have got on fine so far. Why the need for change?"

An influential member of the Congressional committee which was considering the subject of benefits to veterans was even more outspoken in his opposition. "What you are arguing for," he said, "is to spend more public money on a selected student who wants to study law or medicine than on some other fellow. That is socialism, and I'm against it!" The G.I. law, as finally enacted, contained no selective features. The length of education financed by the government depended on the length of military service by the veteran. An equitable provision in some ways and one easy to administer, but not necessarily the best way of spending federal funds to fill that gap of trained people which the war had caused.

The reactions I have just described were by no means atypical. Rather they represent opinions frequently expressed in the 1920's and 1930's. I think it fair to say that, up to the end of World War II, there was little enthusiasm in the United States for an expansion of scholarships for able students. To be sure, in a number of privately endowed colleges special scholarship funds had existed for many years. But the number of students benefiting from these endowments was not large, and rarely if ever was the amount of the award sufficient to cover all the expenses of the college year. The successful applicant counted himself fortunate if the stipend received covered the tuition and the room rent. Either assistance from the family or money earned was needed to make both ends meet, and employment during term time or in the summer vacation financed the college education of many, many boys. Those who had thus "worked their way through college" were quite ready to boast of their achievement and correspondingly disinterested in proposals for enlarged scholarship endowments. To those of us who in the depression years argued for more money for scholarships, they tended to reply, "Let the poor but able youth borrow the money and repay the sum with interest over a short period following graduation." And within limits the use of college loan funds had proved to be quite satisfactory.

As one surveys the expansion of public education in the second half of the nineteenth century and the first half of the twentieth, it is evident that the mood of the American people was one of hostility to any differentiation of educational opportunity based on differences in ability. To advocate a selective system of free higher education was to be accused of being undemocratic. Over the years the taxpayers had been slowly brought to the point of supporting high schools and public universities on a scale other countries regarded as gigantic. But the price for the generous support was an unwritten agreement that there should be no discrimination based on intellectual achievement. If some boys and girls were to have a university education at public expense, all (or almost all) must have the same privilege. Just because one man's son was "better at his lessons" than another was no reason, it was said, for him to receive a longer education without cost.

Two characteristically American doctrines appeared to be in conflict—equality of opportunity (the basis of Jefferson's scholarship proposals) and equality of status. The first led to a selective scheme of free higher education; the second implied that, since all vocations were equal, all should require the same length of formal education. The clash of these two ideals, I believe, has determined much of the recent history of American higher education.

I have used the description "characteristically American" for the two doctrines. Yet the idea of equality of opportunity has become today widely accepted in almost all free societies. For us it seems to have a frontier origin, and yet Napoleon paid homage to the same ideal when he said that every soldier in his army carried a field marshal's baton in his knapsack. We can hardly claim to have exclusive possession of the idea that society should be so arranged that a career is open to the talented. The case with the doctrine of equality of status is quite different. Here we are concerned with a notion which in origin and wide acceptance, I would maintain, is strictly American. In the rapidly developing new communities of the West after the Revolution social stratification had not yet occurred. The production and distribution of goods was on a highly individualized basis. A traditional way of regarding one's neighbor was soon established which persists at least in some rural communities to the present day. It was assumed in conversation, at least, that each honest calling was as respectable as all others. The banker or lawyer might make more money than the blacksmith or carpenter, but he was not to be accorded a privileged position. Alexis de Tocqueville recorded in his notebook that

there reigns an unbelievable outward equality in America. All classes are constantly meeting and there does not appear the least arrogance resulting from their different positions. The inequality produced by riches and education are to be found, it is true, in private life. In general the wealthiest and most enlightened live among themselves. But for a stranger the inequalities are not perceptible, and the fact is that they are, I believe, less felt than everywhere else. I don't believe that there is an occupation which by itself lowers the individual therein employed.[22]

The idea of equality of status was thus recognized by a foreign visitor early in the nineteenth century and noted as an American peculiarity. Tocqueville might also have observed the growth of two ideas which were closely related to the doctrine of equality of status. The first was the assumption that anyone who could read and write had sufficient education to serve the country either as an elected or appointed government official. The second was the increasing repugnance to the designation of certain families as indigent and therefore proper recipients of public or private charity.[23] Yet the reader will recall that the selective features of Jefferson's educational proposals were based on premises which were negated by the new popular American notions. The generous provisions for educating a selected few in the proposed grammar schools and a university were justified by Jefferson because those thus educated "at public expense" were prepared for "the care of the public concerns." And only the able boy from a *poor* family was to be the recipient of education at public expense beyond the first three years. Translated into twentieth-century terms, the Jeffersonian selective principle called for generous scholarships for carefully selected students from families too poor to pay for a college preparatory and university education. But Americans instinctively shy away from any scheme that requires a family to produce evidence of its poverty. Even in Great Britain, where in recent years a vast scheme of substantial university scholarships has been in operation, questions are raised as to whether a family's finances should be considered by the public authorities who award the scholarships. The wisdom of what the British call the "means test" has been argued.[24]

One might argue that Jefferson's selective principle was almost totally ignored during the nineteenth and first half of the twentieth century because the principle was in spirit as well as in fact an eighteenth-century proposal: its relevance to American society rapidly vanished as the nineteenth century progressed. There is no doubt that in 1779 Jefferson, in spite of his revolutionary principles, was thinking in terms of a static agrarian and essentially hierarchical society. What he wished to introduce into such a society was what we now call a high degree of "social mobility." He assumed that only a relatively few persons in each state would be involved with the "public concerns." These few, he further assumed, must be well educated. For Jefferson, being well educated meant having a command of Latin, Greek, and French, and a knowledge of at least ancient history, as well as a good prose style and some acquaintance with mathematics. The wealthy planters in Virginia before the American Revolution had been able to provide such education for their sons. With this background many went on and read law with a member of the bar. These were the people who ran the government of Virginia. In the other colonial provinces similarly wellborn individuals were concerned with public affairs. After the Revolution the same sort of people started to run the government of the separate states and of the nation. If Jefferson's education ideas had met with favor and become a reality, the membership of the governing class in Virginia would in each generation have had "to make an opening for the aristocracy of virtue and talent which nature has wisely provided for the direction of the interests of society and scattered with equal hand through all its conditions."

Jefferson justified his proposals on one occasion by arguing that if they were adopted the "worth and genius—from every condition of life," would be able "to defeat the competition of wealth and birth for public trusts." Wonderful phrases, which I admit I never tire of repeating—wonderful phrases, yet tied to a basic eighteenth-century premise, namely, that those who governed would have to be well educated as the eighteenth century understood the term. The others, without grammar school or university education, Jefferson assumed, would rarely if ever become statesmen or even citizens of influence.

Before Jefferson died, American society had taken on a fluidity which was in marked contrast to the rigidity of the society of colonial Virginia or that which characterized Great Britain or the European nations all through the nineteenth century. It was not because of grammar school or university developments, however, that American society became fluid. It was because new opportunities in commerce, industry, and land speculation opened up many careers to the talented who had little formal education. Men of affairs both private and public—businessmen and politicians—were by the middle of the nineteenth century frequently "self-made men." In other words, that "talent which nature had scattered with equal hand" was able, without benefit of higher education, to make a place for itself and run the republic in the decades immediately before and after the Civil War.

In Europe during the nineteenth century a quite different development occurred. The growth of industry required an expansion of government, and this expansion proceeded within the framework of the eighteenth-century hierarchical social structure. To staff the government bureaus and ministries, university graduates were required. For the most part, the public officials were men who had studied in the law faculties. The same course of study was also desirable for a future banker and essential, of course, for a lawyer or future judge. The European universities flourished because they were in fact training citizens for service to the state. Since the pre-university schools and the universities were expensive, something approaching a caste system was perpetuated by the expansion of government and of education. In short, what Jefferson most disliked in colonial Virginia was strengthened and perpetuated by the growth of educational establishments in England, France, Italy, and the Germanic nations. In nineteenth-century America, on the other hand, the highest offices of the state were open to those who had had no benefits of higher education. The national and state governments needed no highly educated civil servants. Indeed, the spoils system after the triumph of Jacksonian democracy almost guaranteed that there would be no trained corps of people to serve the state. To the political victor belonged the political spoils—the appointment of government officials. No aristocracy of birth or wealth put men in a governing position because of the superior education their families had purchased for them. Therefore, there was little need in any state for an educational scheme such as the young Jefferson had envisaged for Virginia. Expanding, industrialized, individualistic America was on the whole a fluid society just because advanced higher education was deemed relatively unimportant.

Where do we stand today? What relevance, if any, have Jefferson's selective principles—in essence scholarship proposals—for the present generation of Americans? Over the years their relevance has been slight indeed. Has the situation radically altered? I believe it has. Furthermore, there are many indications that public opinion is quite different in the 1960's from what it was in 1945. Recently private philanthropy has established and supported substantial national scholarship undertakings, of which the National Merit Scholarship scheme is the most ambitious. Some state legislatures have appropriated money for scholarship awards, and at the postgraduate level federal funds are now widely used to support able students.[25] Signs of a change in the attitude of educators were already evident in the 1930's, but it was a growing recognition of the impact of science and technology on our society which in the 1950's so drastically altered the attitude of so many articulate Americans.

We have long realized that our greatest national asset was the potential talent of each new generation. But only slowly in this century did it become evident that much of this talent was being wasted because a modern industrialized society needs highly talented men and women who have been highly educated. The dramatic proof of such a statement came when the public was informed of what had been the impact of science and technology on weapons and modes of warfare from 1939 to 1945.[26] Concern with national defense and the development of atomic energy soon became concern for the discovery and education of the large number of scientists, engineers, and technicians who must, directly or indirectly, be employed by the federal government. As the nature of the life-and-death competition of the free world with the Sino-Soviet bloc became evident, public demands for improvements in our educational systems resulted in action by the Congress of the United States and by a number of state legislatures. The significance of differentiated education and the public support of especially gifted youth became widely recognized.[27]

While a recognition of the relation of the new technology to modern society and modern weapons has been the driving force behind the radical shift in the attitude of many toward higher education, it is becoming increasingly clear that the kind of world in which we live demands men and women highly educated in the social sciences and the humanities. Furthermore, it is quite impractical to attempt to identify the future scientific leader at an early age. What is required even in terms of manning the vast technical military defense establishment is a flexible scheme of education which favors the development of *all* the talents of the able student. Whether later, through postgraduate study, the youth in question develops his potentialities by the study of law or economics or medicine or science is of secondary significance from the national standpoint. What the nation today requires for its welfare—indeed, for its survival in freedom—is the identification of the most promising of the next generation and their education at public expense.

Has not the wheel come full circle? Jefferson assumed that only university graduates would be involved with the public welfare. For a century and a half or more, this assumption proved to be false in the United States. Today, in a somewhat altered form and for reasons Jefferson never could have suspected, his premise once again is valid. Even leaving aside all arguments which employ such words as "aristocracy" and "democracy," leaving aside the question

61

of the rigidity of our social structure, it is evident to everyone that the United States simply dares not neglect the education of those young people with special intellectual talents.

But should we leave aside the social, the sociological, and the political considerations which the author of the Declaration of Independence had in mind in formulating his educational proposals of 1779? Not according to my view. The fluidity of American society as a fact and a belief in this fluidity as an ideal are essential for the preservation of our faith in the value of our free society. The apparent collision between the doctrines of equality of status and equality of opportunity must be resolved in terms other than those which were dominant in the United States in the nineteenth century.

If I am right in my judgment of our history, it was the absence of any real need for highly educated men that kept American society fluid for so many years. Now that the real need is so apparent, we must endeavor to prevent the consequent changes in our educational institutions from acting as a crystallizing force introducing further rigidity into our social stratification. If we recognize the danger, much can be achieved by the way we formulate our new educational objectives. The wage scale among the great variety of workers needed in our society is so different from what it was even fifty years ago that higher education can no longer be thought of primarily in terms of a ladder to a better income bracket. And the peculiarly American idea still prevails that all forms of honest labor *ought* to be accorded the same social status. Our form of government, with the constant appeals of politicians to a fluid mass of voters, does much to perpetuate this healthy doctrine; so too does the tremendous geographic mobility of the population. What remains to be done is for the media of mass communication and our leaders of opinion to stress the selective principle in education not in terms of a hierarchy of prestige values but in terms of each individual's realizing his own potentialities with consequent benefit to himself *and* to the nation.

Fortunately one stumbling block to the wide acceptance of any scheme of generous grants of public funds to able students has vanished. There is no need for providing, as Jefferson proposed, for board and lodging as well as free instruction for those who have not yet entered a university. The expansion of our public high schools provides free education for youth who live at home. Similarly, for great numbers who live within commuting distance of a free college, there is little or no need for scholarship awards.[28] In some states, at least, it is probably correct to say that almost every boy or girl can in one way or another finance his or her own way through at least the first two years of college. The greatest national need for scholarships (or fellowships, as some prefer to call them) is at the next higher level of instruction. And here the need is urgent. In medicine in particular very little has been done to open careers to those of talent who come from families with little or no money to spare. American mores are now such that it is generally taken for granted that a young man or woman twenty years old or more is expected to be financially independent. Therefore, whether the family be rich or poor makes no difference as far as justifying an award for the support of the able offspring who is an advanced student in a university. The arguments about a "means test" disappear when the scholarship in question is for a selected student in a professional school or in the graduate school of arts and sciences. In other words, the extension upward of free education for all which followed the abolition of the rate bills has enormously simplified the scholarship problem. The need for substantial financial assistance does not now generally arise until the able student is regarded by society as being entirely on his own. The consequent separation of the idea of an award for educational purposes from any suggestion of charitable assistance is a matter of first importance. One difficult element in any public discussion of the merits of a wide scholarship scheme has disappeared.

In these last few pages I have sought to explore the reasons why Jefferson's selective scholarship proposals (his third and fourth objectives) were so long ignored in the United States and why only since World War II has their importance become increasingly recognized. Compared with Great Britain,[29] we are belatedly modifying our educational practices. We are now beginning to set as our goal an educational system through which the future members of the learned professions will be recruited from the able youth irrespective of family income. When we have moved further in the direction we are now headed, we shall have attained an educational posture which is completely Jeffersonian. The acceptance of his selective scholarship proposals (in twentieth-century terms) will have completed a long, slow process, since his other two educational ideals long since won the allegiance of the citizens of this republic.

We have for several generations gloried both in our state universities and in our pattern of universal free education, locally controlled.

It is curious that the almost revolutionary course of world history since 1945, instead of forcing the United States to retreat from Jeffersonian principles, has had just the contrary effect. The relaxed days of the 1920's were followed first by a grim period of depression, then by a frightful war of global dimensions, and finally by our present relentless competition with the Sino-Soviet bloc. Most of this history has been distasteful and unwelcome, some of it tragic and bewildering in its implications. Yet none of the dramatic changes has altered our adherence to the principle of universal public education nor our belief in the need for colleges and universities. Perhaps the most unwelcome change of all, the advent of the fission and fusion bomb and methods of their delivery, has demonstrated the vital necessity for promoting a lengthy education of exceptional men and women wherever found. In short, as I view the American scene of the 1960's, I am ready to declare without hesitation that Jefferson's proposals have become incorporated in the pattern of our educational structure. As to their relevance for the present and the future, one needs to say no more.

Bibliographic Notes

BOYD.

The definitive edition of Jefferson's papers is now in process of publication by the Princeton University Press. Volume XVI (November, 1789, to August, 1790) was made available in August, 1961. The series to date has been indexed through Vol. XII. In the future all who are concerned with Jefferson's writings will wish to consult these volumes, which carry the following title: *The Papers of Thomas Jefferson,* Julian P. Boyd, ed. (Princeton, N.J.: Princeton University Press, 195–).

PADOVER.

A convenient source of Jefferson's writings apart from his letters is the one-volume edition assembled by Saul K. Padover, *The Complete Jefferson* (New York: Duell, Sloan and Pearce, 1943).

LIPSCOMB.

One of the older standard collections of Jefferson's papers, including many but by no means all of his letters, is the set of 20 volumes carrying the title: *The Writings of Thomas Jefferson,* Monticello Edition, Andrew A. Lipscomb and Albert E. Bergh, eds. (Washington, D.C.: Thomas Jefferson Memorial Association, 1904).

CABELL.

For the history of the founding of the University of Virginia and Jefferson's views on education after 1813, the collection of the correspondence between Jefferson and Joseph C. Cabell is invaluable. The full title is *Early History of the University of Virginia as Contained in the Letters of Thomas Jefferson and Joseph C. Cabell* (Richmond, Va.: T. W. Randolph, 1856).

A recently published (1961) collection of Jefferson's writings will be of special interest to educators. *Crusade Against Ignorance: Jefferson on Education,* Gordon C. Lee, ed., is No. 6 in the Columbia University Teachers College series, Classics on Education. The anthology covers a much wider field than I have attempted and includes extracts from some of Jefferson's political papers, those dealing with religious freedom as well as some concerned with education.

65

It is interesting to note that the first publication of Jefferson's papers, edited by Thomas Jefferson Randolph in 1829 (four volumes, Charlottesville, Va.), does not contain the texts of Jefferson's bills of 1779 or of 1817–1818, and "education" is not given as an index entry. The autobiographical fragment which very briefly describes his 1779 proposals would be a reader's only clue to Jefferson's concern with public education. The second collected edition (edited by H. A. Washington and published in 1853–1854) likewise failed to provide details of Jefferson's first attempt to reform Virginia education and gave only an incomplete account of his second attempt. Apparently not until the 1890's were the texts of bill 79 and 80 of 1779 readily available. They were printed by P. L. Ford in *The Writings of Thomas Jefferson* (10 volumes, 1892–1899). For many years after Jefferson's death the only easily accessible information about his educational proposals was to be found in his autobiography, his *Notes on Virginia,* and in a pamphlet circulated in Virginia in 1818 containing his plan of 1817. It is very much of a question, however, whether this pamphlet would have come to the attention of Barnard and Mann and other reformers of the 1830's and 1840's. Even the publication of the Jefferson-Cabell letters in 1856 shed little light on Jefferson as an educational innovator of 1779. Rather, this book focused attention on Jefferson's role in the founding of the University of Virginia. There would seem to be a problem here which deserves further study: To what extent were those interested in educational reform in the period 1825–1890 aware of the scope of Jefferson's ideas?

Honeywell.
The Educational Work of Thomas Jefferson by Roy J. Honeywell (Cambridge, Mass.: Harvard University Press, 1931) is the only comprehensive scholarly account of Jefferson's lifelong concern with schools and universities. In his Appendixes Honeywell published some of the more important of Jefferson's papers dealing with education.

The first book dealing primarily with Jefferson's ideas on education seems to have been that of John Cleaves Henderson, *Thomas Jefferson's Views on Public Education* (New York and London: G. P. Putnam's Sons, 1890). The focus of attention is Jefferson's part in founding the University of Virginia.

The Free School Idea in Virginia Before the Civil War by William A. Maddox (New York: Columbia University Press, 1918), contains much valuable material.

Bibliographic Notes

The Jefferson Image in the American Mind, Merill D. Peterson (New York: Oxford University Press, 1960) traces the fate of Jefferson's ideas and his reputation through the nineteenth and into the twentieth century. Relatively little space is devoted to Jefferson's educational proposals. There is an extensive bibliography of great value.

Notes

CHAPTER 1

1. William A. Maddox, *The Free School Idea in Virginia Before the Civil War* (New York: Columbia University Press, 1918) gives a detailed account of the various attempts to establish a system of free public schools in Virginia before the Civil War. In my second chapter I deal with the second phase of Jefferson's attempts to establish free schools in his native state.

2. See Appendix I for the text of Bill 79 of 1779 for the "More General Diffusion of Knowledge." The text of this bill is given in Honeywell, Appendix A, pp. 199–205, and in Boyd, vol. II, pp. 526–543. Boyd's text differs from Honeywell's in several minor respects including the absence of numbered sections. Bill 79, though printed on June 18, 1779, was introduced along with many other bills late in 1778. See Boyd, vol. II, pp. 305–324, 535. Much of the proposed legislation for "Revisal of the Laws" was delayed for final consideration until 1785 and 1786. Bill 79 was presented for the second time on June 12, 1780, but no action was taken. In October, 1785, Madison presented it again with other bills, and it was considered by the House of Delegates in December, amended, and passed with a new title, but died in the Senate a year later. Madison wrote to Jefferson in Paris about the bill on December 4, 1786 (Boyd, vol. X, pp. 575–576) as follows:

   The bill on the subject of Education, which could not safely be brought into discussion at all last year, has undergone a pretty indulgent consideration this. In order to obviate the objection of the inability of the County to bear the expense, it was proposed that it should be passed into a law, but its operation suspended for three or four years. Even in this form, however, there would be hazard in pushing it to a final question, and I begin to think it will be best to let it lie over for the supplemental Revisors, who may perhaps be able to put it into some shape that will lessen the objection of expense.

3. *Notes on the State of Virginia.* Queries XIV and XV, Padover, pp. 667–670. For text of the relevant portions of the *Notes,* see Appendix II.

4. See Appendix I for full text of the bill.

5. Appendix I, Sect. XVIII of Bill 79.

6. Appendix I, Sect. XIX of Bill 79.

7. Charles Warren, *The Making of the Constitution* (Boston: Little, Brown, 1937), pp. 399–403, writes as follows in summarizing the discussion in the Constitutional Convention (Wed., Aug. 8, 1787) as to the qualification of voters:

   Every state required a certain length of residence; Maryland and Virginia excluded free Negroes; all the States required an elector to own a certain amount of property, except Pennsylvania, Georgia and New Hampshire which allowed taxpayers to vote. The property qualifications varied greatly; some States required him to own a freehold in a certain number of acres, or in land paying a certain income; New Jersey required ownership of fifty pounds of property of any kind. Freehold in fifty acres was the maximum qualification as to land; and ownership of sixty pounds' worth of other property, the maximum as to personality. It has been estimated that about one fifth of the adult white males possessed no vote.

Vermont entered the Union in 1791 and was at that time a frontier Western state. The constitution of the state provided for universal male suffrage. Frederick Jackson Turner in his *Frontier in American History* (New York: Henry Holt, 1921) attributed the spread of universal male suffrage to the influence of the West. He wrote (pp. 250–252):

All of these scattered democratic tendencies Jefferson combined, in the period of Washington's presidency, into the Democratic-Republican Party. Jefferson was the first prophet of American democracy. . . . Simplicity and economy in government, the right of revolution, the freedom of the individual, the belief that those who win the vacant lands are entitled to shape their own government in their own way—these are all parts of the platform of political principles to which he gave his adhesion, and they are all elements eminently characteristic of the Western democracy into which he was born. . . .

Nevertheless Thomas Jefferson was the John the Baptist of democracy, not its Moses. Only with the slow setting of the tide of settlement farther and farther toward the interior did the democratic influence grow strong enough to take actual possession of the government. The period from 1800 to 1820 saw a steady increase in these tendencies. . . . New England Federalism looked with a shudder at the democratic ideas of those who refused to recognize the established order. But in that period there came into the Union a sisterhood of frontier States—Ohio, Indiana, Illinois, Missouri— *with provisions for the franchise that brought in complete democracy.* [Italics mine.—J. B. C.]

Even the newly created States of the Southwest showed the tendency. The wind of democracy blew so strongly from the West, that even in the older States of New York, Massachusetts, Connecticut, and Virginia, conventions were called which liberalized their constitutions by strengthening the democratic basis of the state.

8. Full text in Appendix II.
9. The letters are given in Appendixes III and IV; Boyd, vol. X, p. 245, and vol. IX, p. 150.
10. See Claude G. Bowers, *Jefferson and Hamilton* (Boston: Houghton Mifflin, 1925), and John C. Miller, *Alexander Hamilton* (New York: Harper, 1959). For Jefferson's own views of the political transformations around 1800, see the skillfully edited collection of Jefferson's papers entitled *Jefferson Himself,* Bernard Mayo, ed. (Boston: Houghton Mifflin, 1947). See note 7 above for F. J. Turner's views as to Jefferson's influence on the extension of suffrage.
11. The relevant portions of the bill are printed in Appendix XV of this volume. Honeywell, Appendix H, pp. 233–243, gives the text as derived from Cabell, pp. 413–427 and pp. 96–98.
12. Section 6 of the bill as sent to Mr. Scott, Chairman of the Committee of Schools and Colleges, Virginia Legislature, 1817–1818, did not contain the second sentence. This had been omitted on the advice of Col. W. C. Nicholas and many others; it is given in Cabell, p. 96, as is Jefferson's note. (See Appendix XV of the present book.) The reference to the Spanish Cortes is in a letter to DuPont de Nemours, April 24, 1816 (Lipscomb, vol. XIV, p. 491), in which Jefferson writes as follows: "In the Constitution of Spain, as proposed by the late Cortes, there was a principle entirely new to me, and not noticed in yours, that no person, born after that day, should ever acquire the rights

of citizenship until he could read and write. It is impossible sufficiently to estimate the wisdom of this provision."

13. "We must bear in mind that the primary thought of young Jefferson during those three years [1776–1779] was concentrated consciously on undermining or destroying the whole superstructure of an artificially built and legally maintained aristocracy" (Claude G. Bowers, *The Young Jefferson* [Boston: Houghton Mifflin, 1945]).

14. *The Adams-Jefferson Letters*, L. J. Cappon, ed. (Chapel Hill, N.C.: University of North Carolina Press, 1959), vol. II, pp. 387–392. See Appendix IX. Jefferson refers to this letter in one to J. C. Cabell on Jan. 5, 1815 (Cabell, p. 39; Appendix XII) in which occurs the splendid phrase "what had been proposed here for culling from every condition of our people the natural aristocracy of talents and virtue, and of preparing it by education, at the public expense, for the care of the public concerns." One must note, however, that this was not an accurate statement of what Jefferson had proposed and was later to advocate again. Only the elementary schools were free to all and only the members of the "natural aristocracy" who were *poor* were to receive free education through the university at public expense.

15. See also Jefferson's autobiography, Padover, pp. 1148–1150. The relevant portions are reprinted in Appendix XXV.

16. Herbert B. Adams, *Thomas Jefferson and the University of Virginia*, U.S. Bureau of Education Circular 1 (Washington, D.C.: Government Printing Office, 1888).

17. See Appendix XI; Padover, pp. 1064–1069.

18. See Appendix XV for the relevant portions of the proposals of 1817; Sects. 14–35 deal with the colleges.

19. Appendix XV, Sect. 42. The number of able students to receive scholarships under the 1817 plan is far fewer than under the 1779 proposal. See Honeywell, p. 30, for a detailed comparison.

20. Letter to J. Correa de Serra, Nov. 25, 1817. Lipscomb, vol. XV, pp. 153–157; Appendix XVI. Jefferson no longer advocates history in elementary schools.

21. Honeywell, pp. 51–53, describes Jefferson's last efforts in 1824, 1825, and 1826 on behalf of the colleges.

22. The quotation is from Jefferson's letter to Adams of Oct. 28, 1813. See Appendix IX.

23. Edward H. Reisner, *Nationalism and Education Since 1789* (New York: Macmillan, 1922), p. 121.

24. Some writers have emphasized the influence of French ideas on Jefferson's thinking about education. Of course, after 1784 Jefferson was in close touch with many Frenchmen. His later views on universities (see chap. 2) were undoubtedly shaped to a considerable extent by what he saw in Paris and his correspondence with learned men in France and England. But as a young man Jefferson was not in a position to have learned of any advanced views about education that may have been then circulating in Paris. Indeed, it is more than likely that Jefferson brought to France in 1784 some new ideas about the organization of public instruction, and Condorcet's proposals of 1792 may to some degree have reflected the American's radical doctrines. (For a summary of these and other proposals see Reisner, *op. cit.*)

The idea of grammar schools was, of course, not new. These institutions had existed in England for centuries, and Jefferson must have been aware of their establishment in New England towns in the seventeenth century. Indeed, one can argue that Massachusetts' schools provided the model for Jefferson's scheme. But before he attended the Continental Congress, Jefferson had little opportunity to learn about New England institutions. His admiration for the town meeting as a political device came in later life after, as President, he had encountered New England resistance. Furthermore, the grammar schools of Massachusetts were by no means in a flourishing state in the eighteenth century, and neither then nor later were they conceived as being instruments of revolutionary democracy. No such generous scholarship scheme as Jefferson's had ever been proposed.

25. *Catalogue of the Library of Thomas Jefferson,* E. Millicent Sowerby (Washington, D.C.: Library of Congress, 1952).

26. The connection between Jefferson's selective principle of free education and John Knox's ideas was first pointed out to me by Alexander G. Campbell of Edinburgh during a discussion of education at a seminar held under the auspices of the Salzburg Seminar for American Studies in August, 1959. Considering Jefferson's antipathy to Calvinism, the possibility of his being influenced even indirectly by Knox appeared to me at first remote. On further reflection, however, it seemed that Dr. Small would have talked with young Jefferson about the educational system of Scotland. If he had done so, the radical educational doctrines of the *Book of Discipline* could hardly have been avoided.

27. Andrew Lang, *John Knox and the Reformation* (New York and London: Longmans, Green, 1905), p. 183.

CHAPTER 2

1. In his first proposal of 1779, Jefferson outlined a scheme for awarding what we would call today "a full scholarship for secondary and higher education" on a *competitive* basis for boys from *poor* families. As I shall attempt to make evident in the next chapter, the American people have never taken kindly to competition among youth except in the field of sports. Furthermore there has been a continuing hostility to any designation of one group of families as "poor" and therefore deserving of public charity, even in the form of a scholarship. What the British call a "means test" (a full disclosure of family income) has always met with opposition in the United States, particularly if a local, state, or federal official were involved in such prying into a family's private affairs. (See note 24, chap. 3.) Yet to Jefferson and his contemporaries it was self-evident that there were indigent families and that the children of these families were not receiving an education. Therefore something special needed to be done about it.

The second half of this chapter is concerned with the battle in several states to make "free schools" really free *for all* by abolishing the distinction between those who could afford to pay for schooling and those who could not. The victorious party in this long struggle, I believe, determined the attitude of the American public toward scholarships for many generations. Education at all levels was to be free for *all* in the public schools and the state universities. The costs of living away from home were to be met by a student's "working his way through college." This could be done at a privately endowed college as well as a state university, since the tuition fees until recently were extremely low. The increased interest in expanding the scholarship provisions of certain of the older endowed colleges, particularly in the depression years, drew people's attention to Jefferson's selective principle. This accounts for the fact, I believe, that a number of writers began to refer to Jefferson's interest in training an intellectual aristocracy. Some, including myself, placed in opposition to the Jeffersonian selective principle a Jacksonian concern with education for *all* the people. Roy E. Lieuallen has concluded that such a dichotomy represents a vast oversimplification if not a distortion of American political and social history in the period 1825 to 1850 (Roy E. Lieuallen, "The Jeffersonian and Jacksonian Conceptions in Higher Education," a dissertation, Stanford University, 1954, on deposit in Stanford University). I agree that any identification of the hostile attitude of the American people toward selective scholarships with the outlook of Andrew Jackson or even with the political philosophy of his followers is an error. Furthermore, as I have been at some pains to make evident in the present volume, Jefferson's educational philosophy was multifold; only one of his four objectives can be placed in opposition to the thinking of those who in the late nineteenth and early twentieth century began arguing for "higher education for all." I am indebted to Professor H. W. Cowley of Stanford for calling Dr. Lieuallen's dissertation to my attention.

2. Honeywell should be consulted by all who are particularly interested in Jefferson's role in the founding of the University of Virginia and the development of that institution in the first critical years of its history. See also Herbert B. Adams, *Thomas Jefferson and the University of Virginia*, U. S. Bureau of Education Circular 1 (Washington, D.C.: Government Printing Office, 1888).

   The letters between Jefferson and Cabell are the source from which the historians have freely drawn. The entire collection is well worth reading by anyone deeply concerned with either the early history of the University of Virginia or Jefferson's main preoccupation in the last ten years of his life. The volume is unfortunately not readily available, but some of the more interesting letters have been included in the Appendixes of the present volume.

3. *Notes on Virginia,* Query XV; Appendix II of the present volume.

4. Bill 80 of 1779. The full text is given in Honeywell, Appendix A, pp. 205–210.

5. Honeywell, p. 208.

6. Letter to John Adams, Feb. 6, 1795. *The Adams-Jefferson Letters,* L. J. Cappon, ed. (Chapel Hill, N.C.: University of North Carolina Press, 1959), I, p. 257.

7. Honeywell, Appendix C, pp. 215–216; Appendix VI.

8. H. B. Adams, *op. cit.,* pp. 49–51.

9. Padover, p. 425; Appendix VIII. In view of Jefferson's explicit statement as to the ability of private enterprise to manage so much better than public institutions all the ordinary branches of education, it is surprising to find that some authors have classed Jefferson as an out-and-out supporter of public education from the kindergarten to the university! Of course, one may argue that, as the leader of a political party and President of the United States, Jefferson in this message was throwing a sop to the vested interests in private academies and colleges, which had multiplied since 1779. But I think he was quite sincere and consistent. Any inconsistency resides rather in those who have sought to portray him as the father of universal public education as well as the father of the University of Virginia!

   Jefferson's grammar schools even in 1779 were to be largely supported by tuition, although they were to be established and managed by public officials. As Jefferson observed the growth of private academies and colleges, he might well have felt that what was lacking was free *elementary* education for all on the one hand and a real university on the other. The latter would be so expensive that only public funds could support it. Thus in a sense this message of 1806 foreshadows the position he took in 1817 (see p. 32). What is missing, however, is any evidence of a continuing zeal for "culling the aristocracy of talents and virtue." One wonders why some scholarship proposal which would have sent able poor boys to the private academies and colleges was not furthered by Jefferson during this period of his greatest influence. Possibly Jefferson was more active in this regard than is evident from his papers and correspondence. Certainly the lack of evidence of any national discussion of scholarships or their equivalent in the period 1800 to 1830 shows quite definitely that Jefferson's selective scholarship scheme had failed to arouse popular interest.

In a letter of Feb. 5, 1803 (Lipscomb, vol. X, p. 355; Appendix VII) to Pictet, Jefferson states that he had "still constantly in view to propose to the legislature of Virginia" as large a "seminary of learning" as "our present circumstances would require or bear." This letter indicates that increasingly Jefferson was becoming more interested in a university than in the other parts of his total scheme for education. The educational innovator of 1779 had to some degree lost interest in the most novel parts of his own invention.

10. Letter to Peter Carr of Sept. 7, 1814; Appendix XI. See also his letter of Aug. 25, 1814, to Thomas Cooper; Appendix X. And see the Report of the Commission (Rockfish Gap Report), Padover, pp. 1097–1105; Honeywell, pp. 248–260; Appendix XVII.

11. Lipscomb, vol. XV, p. 455; Appendix XXIV.

12. "Thus, engrafted upon a bill for the education of the poor, and wrung from a democratic House by a conservative Senate, began the University of Virginia," writes Honeywell, p. 66. For letters between Jefferson and Cabell Feb. 13 to Feb. 22, 1818, see Cabell, pp. 122–127.

13. Appendix XVII.

14. Honeywell, pp. 77–78. The most succinct account of the transformation of Albemarle Academy into the University of Virginia is given in the Introduction to the collection of letters between Jefferson and Cabell (Cabell, p. xxii). For details of the development of the university under Jefferson's guidance, see Honeywell and H. B. Adams.

Albemarle Academy was chartered in 1803 with funds to be raised by a lottery and by private subscription. "The contribution from this source, when once begun, having been both more speedy and liberal than was expected, it was enlarged by the same authority [the legislature] into an institution of higher grade, known as Central College; and before either Academy or College had gone into operation, the latter was adopted by the State, liberally endowed and expanded into the seat of science, now known as the University of Virginia" (Cabell, Introduction, probably by T. W. Randolph, p. xxii). As early as December, 1783, Jefferson had manifested an interest in the establishment of an educational institution near his home. "Just before I left Albemarle," he wrote Cabell, "a proposition was started for establishing there a grammar school. You were so kind as to tell me you would write me the progress of the proposition; on my part I was to enquire for a tutor." Jefferson reports lack of success in this enquiry and suggests it would be best to interest some person in Scotland "to engage a good one. From that country we are surest of having sober, attentive men" (Cabell, p. xxiii). Incidentally, this last sentence shows Jefferson's faith in Scottish education.

15. Cabell, p. 240; see also Cabell, pp. 233–237. For letter dealing with earlier financial troubles, see letters of Jefferson to Cabell and General Breckenridge; Appendixes XIX and XX.

16. Cabell, p. 260; Appendix XXI.

17. Cabell, p. 265.

18. Cabell, p. 268; Appendix XXII. Jefferson's letter in immediate reply is given in Appendix XXIII (Cabell, p. 269).
19. Honeywell, p. 99, quotes Jefferson's letter to William Roscoe, Dec. 27, 1820.
20. The Morrill Act was signed by President Lincoln on July 2, 1862. Its effect on higher education during the next three decades was enormous. The act granted to each state 30,000 acres of public land for each of the state's members of Congress. States having no public lands within their borders received the equivalent in scrip. The land or scrip could be sold and the income from the funds was to support "at least one college where the leading object shall be, without excluding other scientific and classical studies, to teach such branches of learning as are related to agriculture and the mechanic arts." See Richard G. Axt, *The Federal Government and Financing Higher Education* (New York: Columbia University Press, 1952), published for the Commission on Financing Higher Education, chap. ii, pp. 37–50. The state colleges and universities supported in part from the funds thus made available became known as land-grant colleges.
21. Padover, p. 1149; Appendix XXV.
22. W. A. Maddox, *The Free School Idea in Virginia Before the Civil War* (New York: Teachers College, Columbia University, 1918), p. 22. For detailed discussion of the legislative history of Jefferson's and Mercer's proposals as to the use of the Literary Fund during the years 1815–1818 see his chaps. iv and v. Honeywell summarizes this history in two paragraphs (pp. 17–18) of which the concluding sentence reads: "By 1817 Mercer was recognized as the champion of the West, advocating centralized control and indirect support, while Jefferson, through his supporters in the legislature, was equally recognized as the foremost advocate of local control and support." All of which is true but fails to underline the tragedy involved in the failure of Mercer (a Federalist) and his friends to work out with Jefferson's supporters a bill for the establishment of public schools in Virginia. Writing of the questions which faced the legislature in 1815–1817, Maddox sums up his judgment of the complicated history as follows (p. 64):

> In the search for a solution of these puzzling problems, the Mercer and Jefferson factions, reflecting fundamental national party attitudes, had more to fear in each other than in the old fashioned gentlemen who wanted no change but desired no fight. The conservative was in reality in the minority, and had the two factions agreed upon a practical plan of state school administration, there can be no doubt that Virginia would have distinguished herself among the commonwealths.

> For the actual operation of the scheme, which provided state money only for the education of the poor, see Maddox, chap. vi, and Cornelius J. Heatwole, *A History of Education in Virginia* (New York: Macmillian, 1916), pp. 114–116. Those in charge of the expenditure endeavored to find some one who would agree to teach the children of the indigent families. The salary offered was meager, and often no teacher could be found. In this case the tuition at a private school might be paid. It must be remembered that there were few if any public schools in operation. To establish a local school would have cost a good deal.

23. The text of the bill is printed in the Appendix to a pamphlet published in 1826, entitled *A Discourse on Popular Education* by Charles Fenton Mercer (delivered in the Church of Princeton the evening before the annual commencement of the College of New Jersey, Sept. 26, 1826) (Princeton, N.J.: Princeton Press, 1826). Because of the significance of Mercer's bill (which failed by only one vote in setting a pattern for American public education!)

the entire text has been reproduced in the final Appendix (XXVI) of the present volume. Mercer was born in 1778 and graduated from Princeton in 1797. After reading law in Princeton and Richmond, he took up the practice of law in Virginia, his native state. He was a member of the House of Delegates from 1810 to 1817, resigning to take a seat in Congress. During the War of 1812 he was a brigadier-general.

24. Maddox, *op. cit.*, note 22, p. 68; Mercer (*op. cit.*, note 23, p. xiv of his Appendix) stated in 1826 that before the bill passed the House of Delegates, Sect. XXIV, fixing the location of the university, had been altered, "leaving the whole territory of the state open for the site of the university," and he gives his reasons (which are not very convincing) for preferring a location "west of the Blue Ridge." Geographical considerations were certainly involved in the crosscurrents of politics. The west had a majority of the House of Delegates but only four out of twenty-four seats in the Senate (Maddox, p. 68). Jefferson was fixed in his determination to have a university, and in his part of Virginia.

25. Sections II, III, and VIII of Mercer's bill as printed in Appendix XXVI.

26. The Literary Fund had been established by act of the Virginia legislature on Feb. 2, 1810. The sources of funds were forfeitures, legacies, and parish or glebe lands originally set aside by the Crown and now belonging to the state. The purpose was "the encouragement of learning." (Similar funds were established at this period in other states.) The amount was not large but was greatly augmented after the close of the War of 1812 by allocation to it of some $400,000 which had been loaned to the Federal government and was now repaid. This windfall (later increased) was added to the fund by action of the legislature in the session of 1815–1816, and the president and directors of the Literary Fund were required to report a plan for a university and "such additional colleges, academies and schools as shall diffuse the benefits of education throughout the Commonwealth."

According to Mercer (*op. cit.*, note 23, p. xviii) the report of the directors of the Literary Fund was referred to a committee of which he was not a member, and the committee reported several bills which had not been acted on at a late period of the session. Therefore, he was asked by the chairman of the committee to prepare a bill "under great pressure of time." Mercer did so, embodying in his bill "all the suggestions which the mover had submitted to the president and directors of the Literary Fund, along with several which they had rejected." This is the bill which passed the House of Delegates by a large majority (66 to 49) and was defeated in the Senate by a tie vote. Therefore the whole question of how best to "encourage learning" by the use of the augmented Literary Fund went over to the 1817–1818 session. In 1817 a pamphlet entitled "Sundry Documents on the Subject of a System of Public Education" was circulated throughout the state by the order of the legislature. It included both Mercer's and Jefferson's proposals.

One might say that after public opinion in the states had been canvassed, the legislature decided to use the income of the Literary Fund largely for the education of the poor ($45,000) and a small amount ($15,000) for a university whose nature and location was yet to be determined (and about which Jefferson eventually had his way). The editor of the Cabell-Jefferson letters, writing in the 1850's, justifies the passage of the act in 1818 "for the erection of a university and for the education of the poor" with these words, "It was decided not to interfere with education, except in the points where it could not safely be left to individual enterprise, viz.: in the case of persons too poor to pay for it themselves, and in that when the expense and magnitude of the subject defied individual enterprise, as in the case of a University" (Cabell, p. xxviii). From an admirer of Jefferson (at least as father of the University of Virginia), this seems a remarkably complacent account of a great defeat. No word is said about the limitations placed on any scheme by the relatively small size of the Literary Fund. Also in 1826, Mercer makes no mention of this difficulty. Yet he himself must have had worries about the sufficiency of the state money, for early in 1817 the House of Delegates adopted a proposal of his to establish Literary Fund Banks which were to provide eventually for a greatly increased state revenue to be used for education. The bill was killed in the Senate after being assailed by the Republicans (Jeffersonians) (Maddox, pp. 64–66). The usual bitter controversy occurred about government banks, speculation, and stockjobbing, which on the national scene was so frequent in the political discussions of that period. It seems clear that Mercer realized that the state needed a great deal more money if anything like his ambitious scheme was to be put into effect. Lotteries could be used, of course, as they had been occasionally in the past, but would yield only small amounts. Indeed, Mercer's opponents claimed that his Literary Fund Banks (there were to be 23 with capital of seven million dollars) would be in fact a huge lottery.

The more one examines the letters and pamphlets dealing with public education in the United States in the first half of the nineteenth century, the more one is impressed by the financial weakness of the separate states. Politically the states were more than ready to stand up against Federal encroachment. But when it came to paying for a service rendered by the individual states there were neither funds nor accepted procedures for raising funds (except by lotteries). Local property taxes were supposed to take care of local public services, perhaps including local public schools. The Federal government through excise taxes and custom duties was to run a surplus in the 1830's, but the individual state governments were poverty-stricken. This fact must be kept in mind in reviewing not only the fate of Mercer's proposal of 1816–1817 but the history of education in states such as New York and Massachusetts. The recalcitrant taxpayer is a constant figure to be reckoned with in every decade.

One further complication requires mention. In the first quarter of the nineteenth century a new method of teaching children to read, write, and do arithmetic, called the "Lancastrian method," had quite a vogue. It was claimed that by using some of the children as monitors, large classes could be handled very cheaply. Mercer speaks of the experiment with interest. Any way of providing elementary education as low cost would obviously be examined with sympathy by the proponents of free public schools for all.

27. Letter of Nov. 28, 1820. Cabell, pp. 184–186; Appendix XVIII.
28. Mercer, *op. cit.*, note 23, p. 58. The entire section is of interest and is given below:

> Some peculiarities of the New England systems merit, however, if they do not require, in conformity with the end of this discourse, more particular regard. Among these are the total abolition, in the elementary schools, of the odious distinction between the children of the opulent and of the poor, together with the simplicity and utility of that distribution and organization of society, which assures to this system its certain and successful operation.
>
> If it be one of the most salutary effects of popular instruction, to diminish the evils arising to the social order from too great a disparity of wealth, it should be so dispensed as to place the commonwealth with regard to all her children in the relation of a common mother.

A discrimination, therefore, in the same schools, between the children of different parents, which is calculated to implant in very early life, the feelings of humiliation and dependence in one class of society, and of superiority and pride in another, should be avoided as alike incompatible with future harmony and happiness of both.

29. Cabell, pp. 184–187; Appendix XVIII. As Honeywell points out (p. 34) there appears to be "a curious inconsistency" in Jefferson's plans for the financing of the ward schools. His position in his letter of Nov. 28, 1820, is clear and represents acquiescence to the rate-bill system. But four years earlier in his letter of Feb. 2, 1816, to Cabell (Appendix XIII), he had put forward the same idea. The exact words are:

> . . . get them [the people of the ward] to meet and build a log schoolhouse, have a roll taken of the children who would attend it, and of those of them able to pay. These would probably be sufficient to support a common teacher, instructing gratis the few unable to pay. If there should be a deficiency, it would require too trifling a contribution from the county to be complained of. . . .

Yet in the draft bill a year and a half later (see final form of bill in Appendix XV, Sect. 6), Jefferson states that "At this school shall be received and instructed gratis, every infant of competent age who has not already had three years' schooling." (Honeywell, p. 34, believes that Sect. 10 of the same bill is inconsistent with this statement, but I cannot agree with his interpretation of the words of Sect. 10. To me the whole of the bill is consistent and agrees with the position set forth in Bill 79 of 1779.) In a letter of the same year (1817) (Appendix XVI) Jefferson writes: "The expense of the elementary schools for every county, is proposed to be levied on the wealth of the county, and all children rich and poor to be educated at these three years gratis."

It is perhaps significant that when, in 1820, Jefferson comes out so clearly with the proposition that "those of them who are able, paying for the tuition of their own children," he uses language similar to that in his letter of 1816, where he first mentions the same possibility. In both letters he speaks of the inhabitants of the wards building "log houses." My interpretation of his inconsistency on the "rate-bill issue" would be that, when he returned to the consideration of elementary schools in 1814, he realized how strong was the opposition because of the charge on the local taxpayer. Probably aware of what was happening in some other states, he was ready *if need be* to meet the objection by having those who could afford it make a financial contribution for their children's education. That this was a retreat from his original position there could be no doubt. In the debates in 1817–1818 he put forward the point of view he believed in, namely, free education for all. By 1820, however, he was discouraged and was ready to argue for the establishment of elementary schools publicly controlled but largely privately financed.

One must remember that Jefferson was never a proponent of free secondary education for rich and poor alike. His grammar schools (or later district colleges) while publicly controlled were to be largely supported by tuition fees. And he was by no means hostile to private academies or colleges suitably chartered by the state. Indeed, Albemarle Academy was originally just such an institution. See also note 9 above.

30. Andrew S. Draper, *Origin and Development of the Common School System of the State of New York* (Syracuse, N.Y.: C. W. Bardeen, 1903), p. 44. Draper in 1903 was president of the University of Illinois. He had been Superintendent of Public Instruction in New York and in 1890 had delivered an address which was published in revised form in 1903. His account of the rate-bill con-

troversy is of special interest. Speaking in 1890 he could say that every man past fifty could remember the fight for schools free to all. The rate-bill system, he declared, had "become odious."

The best short yet comprehensive account of the historical development of the common school is Lawrence A. Cremin, *The American Common School* (New York: Columbia University Press, 1951).

31. Samuel S. Randall, *The Common School System of the State of New York* (Troy, N.Y.: Johnson and Davis, 1851), p. 72. The quotation is from a portion of the report of Christopher Morgan, Secretary of State and Superintendent of Common Schools of New York for 1848. The report is included in the historical introduction, pp. 5–90.

32. Randall, *op. cit.*, note 32, p. 73. Again the writer is Superintendent Morgan. In the same volume (p. 70) figures are given for 1847, showing that the rate bills collected $466,674, while the amount of public money spent was $639,008.

33. Randall, *op. cit.*, note 32, pp. 74–78. See also Frank T. Carlton, *Economic Influences upon Educational Progress in the United States*, Bulletin of the University of Wisconsin, vol. IV, no. 221 (Madison, 1908). I have followed in general his thesis as to the influence of the cities on educational legislation in New York. The entire article is well worth reading.

34. Draper, *op. cit.*, note 31, p. 51. Among the states using rate bills were Ohio, Michigan, Pennsylvania, New Jersey, Connecticut, and Rhode Island, as well as New York. Francis Adams in a volume entitled *The Free School System of the United States* (London: Chapman and Hall, 1875) reported that "by 1871 the rate-bill system had disappeared throughout the Union."

35. For a detailed description of the history of free education in New York City, see A. Emerson Palmer, *The New York Public School* (New York: Macmillan, 1905). Cremin, *op. cit.*, note 31, pp. 151–175, devotes twenty-four pages to the history of the establishment of the common school in New York City. He brings out the significant role the churches played in the controversy.

36. Palmer, *op. cit.*, note 36, p. 101.

37. Palmer, *op. cit.*, note 36, pp. 140–151 (chap. XVIII).

38. Carlton, *op. cit.*, note 34, p. 77.

39. If one reads through the writings of the leading educators of the period 1825 to 1885, Jefferson's name is hardly mentioned. I have found no recognition of the significance of the details of his proposals except for his connection with the University of Virginia. Because of his attitude toward slavery, he was far from being well regarded in the South, and in New England his activities as President had not endeared him. Writing of the failure of the Embargo Act and the last days of Jefferson's presidency, Henry Adams says, "So complete was his overthrow that his popular influence declined even in the South" (Henry Adams, *The Formative Years: A History of the United States*, condensed by Herbert Agar [Boston: Houghton Mifflin, 1947], vol. II, p. 544). The renaissance of interest in Jefferson seems to have begun in the late nineteenth century. See M. D. Peterson, *The Jefferson Image in the American Mind* (New York: Oxford University Press, 1960). It is only fair to point out that Jefferson's writings on education were not readily available until the publication of his collected works in 1892.

40. Mercer, *op. cit.*, note 23, p. 45, speaking in 1826, said, "It is universally known how much Scotland owes of her past and present happiness to her parish schools . . . but what, when I first learned of it many years ago filled me with astonishment, is, that to Frederick the Great, Prussia was immediately, and a great part of Germany remotely, indebted for a system of popular instruction."

41. See *Reports on European Education*, Edgar W. Knight, ed. (New York: Mc-

Graw-Hill, 1930). The volume contains portions of a translation of Victor Cousin's report and of those of John Griscom and Calvin E. Stowe. Victor Cousin's original report was published in Paris in 1833 as *Rapport sur L'Etat de l'Instruction Publique dans Quelques Pays de l'Allemagne et Particulière-ment en Prusse.*

42. Calvin E. Stowe, *Report on Elementary Public Instruction in Europe Made to the 36th General Assembly of the State of Ohio* (Dec. 19, 1837). Stowe was professor of Biblical literature at the Lane Theological Seminary in Ohio. He had a request from the state legislature, in connection with a trip to Europe he was making for another purpose, to collect "such facts and information as he may deem useful to the state in relation to the various systems of public instruction and education which have been adopted in the several countries through which he may pass. . . ."

For a discussion of Prussian education see Reisner, *Nationalism and Education Since 1789* (New York: Macmillan, 1922), note 26, chap. viii. In his opinion "there was nothing worthy of the name of national education in Prussia up to the time of the reforms that followed upon the Peace of Tilsit" (July, 1807). But the work started by Frederick the Great had impressed at least one American traveler, whose letters about Silesia had inspired Mercer.

43. See note 26 above.

44. Biography of Edmund Dwight, *Dictionary of American Biography* (New York: Scribner's, 1928), vol. V, pp. 563-564.

45. Horace Mann was born in Franklin, Mass., in 1796, graduated from Brown University in 1819; lawyer in Dedham and Boston; member of the Massachusetts House of Representatives 1827-1833, Massachusetts Senate 1833-1837; Secretary of the Board of Education 1838-1848. He was elected to Congress as an anti-slavery Whig in 1848. See *Dictionary of American Biography* (New York: Scribner's, 1928), vol. XII, pp. 240-243, and B. A. Hinsdale, *Horace Mann and the Common School Revival* (New York: Scribner's, 1900).

46. See Cremin, *op. cit.*, note 31, pp. 142-151. See also George H. Martin, *The Evolution of the Massachusetts Public School System* (New York: D. Appleton, 1901), for a general account of the reformation of Massachusetts schools. James G. Carter's *Letters to the Honorable William Prescott LL.D. on the Free Schools of New England* (Boston: Cummings, Hilliard, 1824) and his *Essays upon Popular Education* (Boston: Bowles and Dearborn, 1826), reprinted as Old South Leaflet 135) are of great interest. There is little doubt that Carter was the driving force behind the movement for reform of Massachusetts public schools and in particular for the erection of normal schools for the training of teachers. One of the chief evils which had to be overcome was the extreme decentralization of the local school administration. Within a town there might be a number of districts, each of which was essentially autonomous; often the support and management of the one-room school were far from satisfactory.

47. Interestingly enough, Henry Barnard, like Horace Mann, was a Whig and like Mann was a lawyer by training and a politician by experience. In 1838 he introduced a bill into the Connecticut legislature to provide for a state Board of Education. It was passed, and he reluctantly accepted the position of secretary. Though Connecticut had been a leader in establishing a state fund to support elementary schools (the money came from the sale of its Western Reserve lands in Ohio), education had not prospered. Indeed, some critics thought that the very existence of a generous state allotment discouraged the local people from making the effort they should. The schools were controlled not by the town but by an independent school society which endeavored to live within the budget provided by the state.

Closely paralleling Mann's activities, Barnard addressed himself to the task of presenting the facts to the people of his state. After four years of effective work he was legislated out of office as a result of a state election returning a majority of Democrats to the legislature. On the alleged ground that the results he had attained did not warrant further expenditure of funds, his office was abolished. He then moved to Rhode Island, where his work for public schools was highly effective. When the Whigs recaptured control of the Connecticut legislature, he returned to be Superintendent of Common Schools. See *Dictionary of American Biography* (New York: Scribner's, 1928), vol. I, pp. 621–625, and John S. Brubacher, *Henry Barnard on Education* (New York: McGraw-Hill, 1939).

Barnard's experience in Connecticut indicates how the Democratic party in the 1830's and 1840's carried on the Jeffersonian suspicion of strong centralized government, even government of an individual state. Further evidence on this point is afforded by examining the history of Massachusetts in the same period. In 1839 the Democratic party finally succeeded in electing Marcus Morton governor, and the Whig ascendancy in the legislature was temporarily broken. Morton attacked the new State Board of Education by innuendo in his inaugural address. Then a committee of the legislature on retrenchment, acting on a hint from the governor, recommended the abolition of the State Board, a recommendation adopted by the Committee on Education. A minority report of the committee supporting Mann and the Board was adopted by the House (George H. Martin, *op. cit.*, note 47, pp. 177–178).

48. Carlton, *op. cit.*, note 34, pp. 30–31. For a summary of the extension of suffrage in the various states in the first decades of the nineteenth century and Carlton's evaluation of the influence of this extension on education, see pp. 33–36. He likewise considers the important bearing of the humanitarian movement in Massachusetts (pp. 36–42) and the labor movement (pp. 42–44). Cremin lays great emphasis on these factors.

49. In 1781, Jefferson had written:

Generally speaking, the proportion which the aggregate of the other classes of citizens bears in any state to that of its husbandmen is the proportion of its unsound to its healthy parts, and is a good enough barometer whereby to measure its degree of corruption. While we have land to labor, then, let us never wish to see our citizens occupied at a workbench, or twirling a distaff. Carpenters, masons, smiths are wanting in husbandry; but, for the general operations of manufacture, let our workshops remain in Europe. . . . The mobs of great cities add just so much to the support of pure government, as sores do to the strength of the human body. It is the manners and spirit of a people which preserve a republic in vigor. A degeneracy in these is a canker which soon acts to the heart of its laws and constitutions (*Notes on Virginia*, Query XIX, quoted by Charles A. Beard, *Economic Origins of Jeffersonian Democracy* [New York: Macmillan, 1915], p. 425).

Beard gives it as his opinion that this statement was an "expression of a reasoned conviction based upon an analysis of the economic foundations of democracy."

CHAPTER 3

1. See chap. 2, note 9.
2. See Elmer E. Brown, *The Making of Our Middle Schools* (New York and London: Longmans Green, 1905), chaps. ix and xi.

Notes

3. Brown, *op. cit.*, note 2, p. 241. Brown quotes from George H. Martin, *The Evolution of the Massachusetts Public School System* (New York: D. Appleton, 1894), p. 128, whose third chapter on "The District School and the Academy" should be consulted by those interested in the details of this phase of American educational history.

4. Brown, *op. cit.*, note 2, p. 237.

5. Brown, *op. cit.*, p. 304.

6. Brown, *op. cit.*, p. 713 and Appendix D, p. 519.

7. George S. Boutwell, *Thoughts on Educational Topics and Institutions* (Boston: Phillips, Sampson, 1859), p. 153. The title of the address was "The Relative Merits of Public High Schools and Endowed Academies." It was delivered before the American Institute for Instruction at Manchester, N.H. It is interesting to note that the first compulsory attendance law in the United States was passed by the Massachusetts legislature in Boutwell's first administration (1852). Boutwell, born in 1818, was a Democrat who was elected Governor of Massachusetts as a consequence of a coalition of the Democrats and Free Soilers in 1851 and 1852. He served as Secretary of the Board of Education (1855–1861) and as a member of Congress (1863–1869). He was one of the organizers of the Republican party in Massachusetts in 1855 and as a member of Congress was a "radical Republican." He helped frame the fourteenth and fifteenth amendments (*Dictionary of American Biography*, vol. II, p. 489).

8. Boutwell, *op. cit.*, note 7, pp. 196–197. The title of the address in which these remarks occur is "The High School System," delivered at Bernardston, Mass.

9. Boutwell, *op. cit.*, p. 198. The history of American public education is quite distorted if one overlooks the fact that the public high school was on the one hand free for rich and poor alike and on the other a selective institution, originally more so than the private academies. The revolutionary transformation of the high school took place when in the twentieth century the changed social situation forced these schools to give up their selective feature (see note 18 below). The point is so important that I intrude on the reader a further quotation from George S. Boutwell's discourse on "The High School System," *op. cit.*, p. 199:

> It [a fixed standard of admission] is essential to the true prosperity of this seminary [the public high school], and it is also essential to the intellectual advancement of the people within your influence. You expect pupils from the neighboring towns. Your object is not pecuniary profit, but the education of the people. If your requirements are positive, though it may not be difficult to meet in the beginning, every town that depends on this institution for better learning than it can furnish at home will be compelled to maintain schools of a higher order. . . . Nor let the objection that a rigid standard of qualification will exclude many pupils, and diminish the attendance upon the school, have great weight; for you perform but half your duty when you provide the means of a good education for your own students. You are also, through the power inherent in this authority, to do something to elevate the standard of learning in other schools, and in the county around.

It might be argued that during those years when admission to the public high school was governed by examination (or the satisfactory completion of *all* the work of the first eight grades), these institutions were in effect the equivalent of Jefferson's grammar schools of 1779 and his selective principle was at work. There are three differences between the selective system of public secondary education as it then operated (in many if not all localities) and what Jefferson had proposed. First, the institutions were not residential. But the increased density of the population and improving modes of transportation, it might be said, had made the residential feature unnecessary. Second, the education was free but free for both rich and poor. This meant the extension upwards, so to speak, of what Jefferson had argued for initially for his elementary schools. But this meant that the scheme was far more expensive when calculated in terms of what the poor and able boy was receiving as a benefit. Third, the selection process was far less rigorous than that which Jefferson had contemplated.

Today, in a few large Eastern cities special public high schools (including publicly supported Latin schools) flourish, some of which offer essentially an academic course and have a highly selective admission policy. The proponents of this type of school might well claim to be the true inheritors of the original Jeffersonian selective tradition. But in these schools the children of rich and poor alike have their education paid for by the locality and the state. This has been so for generations, and only goes to underline the reluctance of the American people to inquire into family finances and decide who is indigent and who is not. This reluctance, which developed around the middle of the nineteenth century in connection with the rate-bill controversy, as explained in the last chapter, means of course that far more public funds are expended even in the few selective public high schools than would be the case if Jefferson's original ideas about grammar schools had prevailed. But if they had prevailed we would have an entirely different type of American society! The triumph of the equalitarian democratic spirit which is sometimes associated with the name of Andrew Jackson (see p. 72) long ago set the social framework within which public schools and universities were destined to develop.

10. *Charles E. Stuart and others v. School District No. 1 of the Village of Kalamazoo and Others.* Appeal in Chancery from Kalamazoo Circuit, *Michigan Reports*, vol. 30, pp. 69–85 (Report of cases determined in the Supreme Court of Michigan from July 14, 1874, to January 6, 1875). The full report is reprinted in Edgar W. Knight, *Readings in American Educational History* (New York: Appleton-Century-Crofts, 1951), p. 544.

11. Brown, *op. cit.*, note 2, pp. 365–368, refers with satisfaction to the relation of several state universities to the public schools of the state. At that time (1902) and for twenty-five years or so, the faculty of the University of California sent a professor to inspect the work of the high schools from which students entered the university. In recent years the California inspection system has been replaced by a system in which information is exchanged as to the grades of students in high school and their first year in the university. Accreditation still rests with the university. In Michigan the university no longer accredits.

12. Brown, *op. cit.*, note 2, p. 5.

13. Frank Bunker, *Notes on Reorganization of Public School Systems*, Bulletin 8 of the Bureau of Education, Department of the Interior (Washington, D.C., 1916), pp. 102–110.

14. Brown, *op. cit.*, note 2, p. 480.

15. See chap. 2, note 20.

16. D. C. Gilman was elected President of John Hopkins University on Dec. 29, 1874. The university opened in October, 1876. See B. C. Steiner, *History of Education in Maryland* (Washington, D.C.: U.S. Bureau of Education, 1894). Also D. C. Gilman, *The Launching of a University* (New York: Dodd, Mead, 1906), and Abraham Flexner, *Daniel Coit Gilman* (New York: Harcourt, Brace, 1946).

17. See Earl J. McGrath and Charles H. Russell, *Are Liberal Arts Colleges Becoming Professional Schools?* and E. J. McGrath, *The Graduate School and the De-*

cline of Liberal Education, publications of the Institute of Higher Education of Teachers College, Columbia University, 1958, 1959.

18. The Inglis Lecture, 1959, *The Revolutionary Transformation of the American High School* (Cambridge, Mass.: Harvard University Press, 1959). Also included in James Bryant Conant, *The Child, The Parent, and the State* (Cambridge, Mass.: Harvard University Press, 1959), chap. iv.

19. *Ibid.,* pp. 98–100.

20. "Education for a Classless Society, the Jeffersonian Tradition," *Atlantic Monthly,* vol. 165, pp. 593–602, May, 1940.

21. *Post-War Educational Opportunities for Service Personnel* (Message from the President of the United States Transmitting Preliminary Report of the Armed Forces Committee on Post-War Educational Opportunities for Service Personnel, Oct. 27, 1943. Document 344, House of Representatives, 78th Congress, 1st Session, p. 9).

22. *Tocqueville in America,* George W. Pierson, ed. (New York: Doubleday, 1959), p. 246. Abridged by Dudley C. Lunt from *Tocqueville and Beaumont in America.*

23. See note 1, chap. 2.

24. See Report of the Committee Appointed by the Minister of Education and the Secretary of State for Scotland in June, 1958, entitled "Grants to Students," Presented to Parliament May, 1960 (London: Her Majesty's Stationery Office, Cmnd. 1051), chap. 7, pp. 44–59. The chairman of the committee was Sir Colin Anderson, and the report is commonly known as the Anderson Report. It discusses the procedures by which scholarships and other awards of financial assistance are received by some 83 per cent of the students in the universities (*not* colleges) of Great Britain (see note 28). Since 1946 the principle has been accepted by the public authorities making the awards "that, subject to need, award-holders should be paid the assessed cost of their maintenance and expenses at the university" (p. 2). At present, parents are required to make each year to the award-making authority "a return of their gross income from which various allowances are then deducted"; the result is the basis on which "the amount of the parental contribution is assessed." The grant to the student is paid in full only if the assessed contribution is nil; otherwise the amount of the grant is diminished according to what the authorities have determined as the proper parental contribution and may be extinguished entirely if the assessed contribution is as large as the grant (p. 44).

    The committee report gives in detail the arguments for and against the present practice of assessing a parental contribution. The majority of the members (eleven in number) recommended that "parental contributions should be abolished," and a minority of four recommended "that parental contributions in a modified form should be required." To date (October, 1960) the Minister of Education has not as yet reached a decision on the basic issue. For those who are interested in the general subject of the policy to be pursued in making generous grants to university students, chap. 7 of the Anderson Report is to be recommended.

25. As I prepare this manuscript for the printer (August, 1961), Congress has not yet acted on a bill to provide the scholarship system urged by President Kennedy.

26. The report to the President of the United States, written at the request of President Roosevelt by Vannevar Bush, is a document which had a great influence on postwar thinking, particularly that of members of Congress ("Science the Endless Frontier" [Washington, D.C., 1945]). The establishment of the National Science Foundation was foreshadowed in this report, which dealt

with both the need for federal funds for research and the need of financial support for university students. An appendix proposing a wide-scale system of federal scholarships is of special interest. The document was reprinted in July, 1960, by the National Science Foundation, Washington, D.C., with an interesting introduction by Alan T. Waterman.

27. As evidence of the changed attitude toward scholarships, one might cite the establishment in 1955 of the National Merit Scholarship Corporation with an initial grant of 20 million dollars from the Ford Foundation and a grant of $500,000 from the Carnegie Corporation. Scholarship awards are given on a competitive regional basis to selected students entering a four-year undergraduate course. In 1959, 920 scholars received awards from the Corporation at an estimated value of 3.7 million dollars. Over the period 1956–1959 inclusive, 3,465 scholars received awards at an estimated value of 15.5 million dollars. Some 90 business and industrial corporations are now involved in the program, providing a major share of the financial burden.

28. In almost all metropolitan areas of the United States tuition-free education at the undergraduate level is available either through state or municipal institutions. In the other areas private institutions provide instruction at a relatively low cost because the student lives at home. (It is the expense of room and board which makes college education so expensive in many residential colleges.) Since our labor laws and employment practices make it difficult if not impossible for boys and girls of high school age to obtain full-time employment, society expects the family to provide food and shelter at least until the offspring are eighteen or nineteen, and longer if they are attending college. (The contrast with Great Britain and European countries is marked in this respect. In societies where families count on the earning power of boys over fourteen years of age, the question of a public compensation for the loss of family income arises if the youth attends school full-time even if there is no tuition charge. I have never heard this issue raised in the United States.)

The most economical form of undergraduate education is that provided locally, and the spread of the two-year local community college (junior college) is testimony to the recognition of this principle by the American taxpayer. In California, the state, through legislative action, has established a flexible system of public education beyond the high school which involves three types of institutions: two-year junior colleges, four-year state colleges, and a number of campuses of the University of California. Transfer from one type of college to another is encouraged. For example, a student who completes two years of academic work in a junior college may enter the junior year at the University provided he meets certain standards. The scheme provides opportunity for the "late bloomer" who is university material, as well as a two-year technical education for many. In states where such a flexible and widespread system of free education is available, the financial barriers to a college education are so slight that few if any able youth fail for financial reasons to go on with education beyond the high school. The need for assistance in the form of generous scholarships is at the next level of higher education.

29. The British can claim that, since the end of World War II, their educational system has become very similar to what Jefferson proposed except for the fact that the grammar schools are for the most part local and not residential. The road to the university—a European university, *not* an undergraduate college —this road is open to the poor but able boy and girl. Over 80 per cent of all the university students now receive some financial help from the state (see note 24). To what degree family tradition hinders the acceptance of the opportunity thus offered by the state is another matter. Certainly many families never

think of trying to enroll even the ablest of their children in the pre-university schools. In these cases family tradition, which plays so large a role in Great Britain, indicates some way of earning a living other than the practice of a profession.

Taking England and Wales as a whole, one finds from the figures given in the Report of the Ministry of Education for 1959 that about 4 per cent of the age group enters a university. But this is an average figure; in some localities the figure is as high as 16 per cent, in others as low as 2 per cent. (See scholarship and other awards by counties and county boroughs as well as school attendance figures for pupils aged 17 in "Selected Statistics Relating to Local Education Authorities in England and Wales for 1957–58" [Her Majesty's Stationery Office, London, 1959].) The reader will remember that, as compared with the American undergraduate college, the universities in Great Britain are concerned with specialized academic education, and furthermore, with few exceptions those who wish to enter a university must attend a grammar school (tuition-free) or its equivalent; entry into these pre-university schools is made at age 11 plus by those who succeed in passing the entrance examination (the nation over, something like 15 per cent of an age group are enrolled in such schools). The "sixth form" of the grammar school constitutes a two- or three-year course in which a high degree of specialization occurs to prepare the student to obtain the necessary standing on the General Certificate of Education examinations in order to be accepted by the university of his or her choice. In the academic year 1958–1959 there were approximately 100,000 students in the universities of Great Britain, of whom 79,000 were students from the United Kingdom studying for the first degree. Of the latter 65,422 held awards from public funds at a cost to the British taxpayer of 16.8 million pounds. During the next few years it is planned to increase the number of places in the university so that the number of first-degree students will reach about 107,000. If this is done and the scale of the awards continued, the total annual cost will be about 34 million pounds, or approximately 100 million dollars. (If the United States with approximately four times as large an age group were to spend an equivalent amount for university scholarships, the figure would be not far from half a billion dollars.) The amount of public funds spent in Great Britain on the education of youth beyond fourteen years of age who are *not* going to attend a university is very small compared to the United States. It is clear that by the mid-twentieth century the British and the American educational schemes had evolved in such a way as to represent very different allocations of the tax receipts used for education of youth.

The British tradition of generous scholarship grants is an old one. In Scotland for generations the poor but able boy has been able to win a bursary to enable him to attend a university. Oxford and Cambridge have had some scholarships available on a competitive basis for years. As the newer universities developed, some scholarships there were made available. A "means test" was accepted until recently without question. None of the American repugnance to charity awards seems to have been present, and the tradition of working one's way through college certainly has never developed. The vast expansion of the scholarship scheme for university students, however, is a post-World War II phenomenon. It should be noted that the universities (which in comparison with the United States are few in number) are given the power to determine who shall be admitted and who shall not. The national policy is that all who are admitted shall be able to continue their education subsidized to the extent necessary by the state. At present the enrollments are limited by the facilities and staff available. Therefore, university education the nation over is on a highly competitive basis. As the staff and facilities are expanded, the point will presumably come when this will no longer be so and when entrance to the least popular university will be determined by standards set by the faculty in terms of the intellectual promise of the student. It will be interesting to see, when this point is reached, what percentage of an age group will be enrolled in university courses (or their equivalent) and thus the recipients of public subsidy.

Appendixes

Extracts from some of the more important of Jefferson's writings about education are printed in the following pages to give the reader a glimpse of the evolution of Jefferson's ideas about schools and universities as expressed in his own language. With the exception of the bills which are couched in legal terms and contain a confusing mass of details, the other extracts are easy reading. All the letters except one (Appendix XXII) are from Jefferson. Many contain delightful and famous phrases.

As the final item (Appendix XXVI) I have reproduced in full the text of the bill introduced into the Virginia legislature by Charles F. Mercer in 1817 and passed by the House of Delegates. I have done so because the proposed legislation is so little known and the volume in which it is printed is not easily accessible.

APPENDIX I

BILL 79 OF 1779 FOR THE
"MORE GENERAL DIFFUSION OF KNOWLEDGE"

(Honeywell, pp. 199–205; Boyd, pp. 526–543)

SECT. I. Whereas it appeareth that however certain forms of government are better calculated than others to protect individuals in the free exercise of their natural rights, and are at the same time themselves better guarded against degeneracy, yet experience hath shown, that even under the best forms, those entrusted with power have, in time, and by slow operations, perverted it into tyranny; and it is believed that the most effectual means of preventing this would be, to illuminate, as far as practicable, the minds of the people at large, and more especially to give them knowledge of those facts, which history exhibiteth, that, possessed thereby of the experience of other ages and countries, they may be enabled to know ambition under all its shapes, and prompt to exert their natural powers to defeat its purposes; And whereas it is generally true that that people will be happiest whose laws are best, and are best administered, and that laws will be wisely formed, and honestly administered, in proportion as those who form and administer them are wise and honest; whence it becomes expedient for promoting the publick happiness that those persons, whom nature hath endowed with genius and virtue, should be rendered by liberal education worthy to receive, and able to guard the sacred deposit of the rights and liberties of their fellow citizens, and that they should be called to that charge without regard to wealth, birth or other accidental condition or circumstance; but the indigence of the greater number disabling them from so educating, at their own expense, those of their children whom nature hath fitly formed and disposed to become useful instruments for the public, it is better that such should be sought for and educated at the common expense of all, than that the happiness of all should be confined to the weak or wicked:

SECT. II. Be it therefore enacted by the General Assembly, that in every county within this commonwealth, there shall be chosen annually, by the electors qualified to vote for Delegates, three of the most honest and able men of their county, to be called the Aldermen of the county; and that the election of the said Aldermen shall be held at the same time and place, before the same persons and notified and conducted in the same manner as by law is directed, for the annual election of Delegates for the county.

SECT. III. The person before whom such election is holden shall certify to the court of the said county the names of the Aldermen chosen, in order that the same may be entered of record, and shall give notice of their election to the said Aldermen within a fortnight after such election.

SECT. IV. The said Aldermen on the first Monday in October, if it be fair, and if not, then on the next fair day, excluding Sunday, shall meet at the court-house of their county, and proceed to divide their said county into hundreds, bounding the same by water courses, mountains, or limits, to be run and marked, if they think necessary, by the county surveyor, and at the county expence, regulating the size of the said hundreds, according to the best of their discretion, so as that they may contain a convenient number of children to make up a school, and be of such convenient size that all the children within each hundred may daily attend the school to be established therein, and distinguishing each hundred by a particular name; which division, with the names of the several hundreds, shall be returned to the court of the county and be entered of record, and shall remain unaltered until the increase or decrease of inhabitants shall render an alteration necessary, in the opinion of any succeeding Alderman, and also in the opinion of the court of the county.

SECT. V. The electors aforesaid residing within every hundred shall meet on the third Monday in October after the first election of Aldermen, at such place, within their hundred, as the said Aldermen shall direct, notice thereof being previously given to them by such person residing within the hundred as the said Aldermen shall require who is hereby enjoined to obey such requisition, on pain of being punished by amercement and imprisonment. The electors being so assembled shall choose the most convenient place within their hundred for building a school-house. If two or more places, having a greater number of votes than any others, shall yet be equal between themselves, the Aldermen, or such of them as are not of the same hundred, on information thereof, shall decide between them. The said Aldermen shall forthwith proceed to have a school-house built at the said place, and shall see that the same shall be kept in repair, and, when necessary, that it be rebuilt; but whenever they shall think necessary that it be rebuilt, they shall give notice as before directed, to the electors of the hundred to meet at the said school-house, on such a day as they shall appoint, to determine by vote, in the manner before directed, whether it shall be rebuilt at the same, or what other place in the hundred.

SECT. VI. At every of those schools shall be taught reading, writing, and common arithmetick, and the books which shall be used therein for instructing the children to read shall be such as will at the same time make them acquainted with Graecian, Roman, English, and American history. At these schools all the free children, male and female, resident within the respective hundred, shall be intitled to receive tuition gratis, for the term of three years, and as much longer, at their private expense, as their parents, guardians, or friends shall think proper.

SECT. VII. Over every ten of these schools (or such other number nearest thereto, as the number of hundreds in the county will admit, without fractional divisions) an overseer shall be appointed annually by the Aldermen at their first meeting, eminent for his learning, integrity, and fidelity to the commonwealth, whose business and duty it shall be, from time to time, to appoint a teacher to each school, who shall give assurance of fidelity to the commonwealth, and to remove him as he shall see cause; to visit every school once in every half year at the least; to examine the scholars; see that any general plan of reading and instruction recommended by the visiters of William and Mary College shall be observed; and to superintend the conduct of the teacher in everything relative to his school.

SECT. VIII. Every teacher shall receive a salary of ———— by the year, which, with the expences of building and repairing the school-houses, shall be provided in such manner as other county expences are by law directed to be provided and shall also have his diet, lodging, and washing found him, to be levied in like manner, save only that such levy shall be on the inhabitants of each hundred for the board of their own teacher only.

SECT. IX. And in order that grammer schools may be rendered convenient to the youth in every part of the commonwealth, be it therefore enacted, that on the first Monday in November, after the first appointment of overseers for the hundred schools, if fair, and if not, then on the next fair day, excluding Sunday, after the hour of one in the afternoon, the said overseers appointed for the schools in the counties of Princess Ann, Norfolk, Nansemond, and Isle-of-Wight, shall meet at Nansemond court-house; those for the counties of Southampton, Sussex, Surry and Prince George, shall meet at Sussex court-house; those for the counties of Brunswick, Mecklenburg and Lunenburg, shall meet at Lunenburg court-house; those for the counties of Dinwiddie, Amelia and Chesterfield, shall meet at Chesterfield court-house; those for the counties of Powhatan, Cumberland, Goochland, Henrico and Hanover, shall meet at Henrico court-house; those for the counties of Prince Edward, Charlotte and Halifax, shall meet at Charlotte court-house; those for the counties of Henry, Pittsylvania and Bedford, shall meet at Pittsylvania court-house; those for the counties of Buckingham, Amherst, Albemarle and Fluvanna, shall meet at Albemarle court-house; those for the counties of Botetourt, Rockbridge, Montgomery, Washington and Kentucky, shall meet at Botetourt court-house; those for the counties of Augusta, Rockingham and Greenbriar, shall meet at Augusta court-house; those for the counties of Accomack and Northampton, shall meet at Accomack court-house; those for the counties of Elizabeth City, Warwick, York, Gloucester, James City, Charles City and New-Kent, shall meet at James City court-house; those for the counties of Middlesex, Essex, King and Queen, King William and Caroline, shall meet at King and Queen court-house; those for the counties of Lancaster, Northumberland, Richmond and Westmoreland, shall meet at Richmond court-house; those for the counties of King George, Stafford, Spotsylvania, Prince William and Fairfax, shall meet at Spotsylvania court-house; those for the counties of Loudoun and Fauquier, shall meet at Loudoun court-house; those for the counties of Culpeper, Orange and Louisa, shall meet at Orange court-house; those for the county of Shenandoah and Frederick, shall meet at Frederick court-house; those for the counties of Hampshire and Berkeley, shall meet at Berkeley court-house; and those for the counties of Yohogania, Monongalia, and Ohio, shall meet at the Monongalia court-house; and shall fix on such place in some one of the counties in their district as shall be most proper for situating a grammer school-house, endeavoring that the situation be as central as may be to the inhabitants of the said counties, that it be furnished with good water, convenient to plentiful supplies of provision and fuel, and more than all things that it be healthy. And if a majority of the overseers present should not concur in their choice of any one place proposed, the method of determining shall be as follows: If two places only were proposed, and the votes be divided, they shall decide between them by fair and equal lot; if more than two places were proposed, the question shall be put on those two which on the first division had the greater number of votes; or if no two places had a greater number of votes than the others, then it shall be decided by fair and equal lot (unless it can be agreed by a majority of votes) which of the places having equal numbers shall be thrown out of the competition, so that the question shall be put on the remaining two, and if on this ultimate question the votes shall be equally divided, it shall then be decided finally by lot.

SECT. X. The said overseers having determined the place at which the grammer school for their district shall be built, shall forthwith (unless they can otherwise agree with the proprietors of the circumjacent lands as to location and price) make application to the clerk of the county in which the said house is to be situated, who shall thereupon issue a writ, in the nature of a writ of ad quod damnum, directed to the sheriff of the said county commanding him to summon and impannel twelve fit persons to meet at the place, so destined for the grammer school-house, on a certain day, to be named in the said writ, not less than five, nor more than ten, days from the date thereof; and also to give notice of the same to the proprietors and tenants of the lands to be viewed if they be found within the county, and if not, then to their agents therein if any they have. Which freeholders shall be charged by the said sheriff impartially, and to the best of their skill and judgment to view the lands round about the said place, and to locate and circumscribe, by certain meets and bounds, one hundred acres thereof, having regard therein principally to the benefit and convenience of the said school, but respecting in some measure also the convenience of the said proprietors, and to value and appraise the same in so many several and distinct parcels as shall be owned or held by several and distinct owners or tenants, and according to their respective interests and estates therein. And after such location and appraisement so made, the said sheriff shall forthwith return the same under the hands and seals of the said jurors, together with the writ, to the clerk's office of the said county and the right and property of the said proprietors and tenants in the said lands so circumscribed shall be immediately devested and be transferred to the commonwealth for the use of the said grammer school, in full and absolute dominion, any want of consent or disability to consent in the said owners or tenants notwithstanding. But it shall not be lawful for the said overseers so to situate the grammer school-house, nor to the said jurors so to locate the said lands, as to include the mansion-house of the proprietor of the lands, nor the offices, curtilage, or garden, thereunto immediately belonging.

SECT. XI. The said overseers shall forthwith proceed to have a house of brick or stone, for the said grammer school, with necessary offices, built on the said lands, which grammer school-house shall contain a room for the school, a hall to dine in, four rooms for a master and usher, and ten or twelve lodging rooms for the scholars.

SECT. XII. To each of the said grammer schools shall be allowed out of the public treasury, the sum of ———— pounds, out of which shall be paid by the Treasurer, on warrant from the Auditors, to the proprietors or tenants of the lands located, the value of their several interests as fixed by the jury, and the balance thereof shall be delivered to the said overseers to defray the expense of the said buildings.

Sect. XIII. In either of these grammer schools shall be taught the Latin and Greek languages, English Grammer, geography, and the higher part of numerical arithmetick, to wit, vulgar and decimal fractions, and the extrication of the square and cube roots.

Sect. XIV. A visiter from each county constituting the district shall be appointed, by the overseers, for the county, in the month of October annually, either from their own body or from their county at large, which visiters, or the greater part of them, meeting together at the said grammer school on the first Monday in November, if fair, and if not, then on the next fair day, excluding Sunday, shall have power to choose their own Rector, who shall call and preside at future meetings, to employ from time to time a master, and if necessary, an usher, for the said school, to remove them at their will, and to settle the price of tuition to be paid by the scholars. They shall also visit the school twice in every year at the least, either together or separately at their discretion, examine the scholars, and see that any general plan of instruction recommended by the visiters, of William and Mary College shall be observed. The said masters and ushers, before they enter on the execution of their office, shall give assurance of fidelity to the commonwealth.

Sect. XV. A steward shall be employed, and removed at will by the master, on such wages as the visiters shall direct; which steward shall see to the procuring provisions, fuel, servants for cooking, waiting, house cleaning, washing, mending, and gardening on the most reasonable terms; the expence of which, together with the steward's wages, shall be divided equally among all the scholars boarding either on the public or private expence. And the part of those who are on private expence, and also the price of their tuitions due to the master or usher, shall be paid quarterly by the respective scholars, their parents, or guardians, and shall be recoverable, if withheld, together with costs, on motion in any Court of Record, ten days notice thereof being previously given to the party, and a jury impannelled to try the issue joined, or enquire of the damages. The said steward shall also, under the direction of the visiters, see that the houses be kept in repair, and necessary enclosures be made and repaired, the accounts for which, shall, from time to time, be submitted to the Auditors, and on their warrant paid by the Treasurer.

Sect. XVI. Every overseer of the hundred schools shall, in the month of September annually, after the most diligent and impartial examination and inquiry, appoint from among the boys who shall have been two years at the least at some one of the schools under his superintendance, and whose parents are too poor to give them farther education, some one of the best and most promising genius and disposition, to proceed to the grammer school of his district; which appointment shall be made in the court-house of the county, and on the court day for that month if fair, and if not, then on the next fair day, excluding Sunday, in the presence of the Aldermen, or two of them at the least, assembled on the bench for that purpose, the said overseer being previously sworn by them to make such appointment, without favor or affection, according to the best of his skill and judgment, and being interrogated by the said Aldermen, either on their own motion, or on suggestions from the parents, guardians, friends, or teachers of the children, competitors for such appointment; which teachers the parents shall attend for the information of the Aldermen. On which interrogatories the said Aldermen, if they be not satisfied with the appointment proposed, shall have right to negative it; whereupon the said visiters may proceed to make a new appointment, and the said Aldermen again to interrogate and negative, and so toties quoties until an appointment be approved.

SECT. XVII. Every boy so appointed shall be authorized to proceed to the grammer school of his district, there to be educated and boarded during such time as is hereafter limited; and his quota of the expences of the house together with a compensation to the master or usher for this tuition, at the rate of twenty dollars by the year, shall be paid by the Treasurer quarterly on warrant from the Auditors.

SECT. XVIII. A visitation shall be held, for the purpose of probation, annually at the said grammer school on the last Monday in September, if fair, and if not, then on the next fair day, excluding Sunday, at which one third of the boys sent thither by appointment of the said overseers, and who shall have been there one year only, shall be discontinued as public foundationers, being those who, on the most diligent examination and enquiry, shall be thought to be the least promising genius and disposition; and of those who shall have been there two years, all shall be discontinued save one only the best in genius and disposition, who shall be at liberty to continue there four years longer on the public foundation, and shall thence forward be deemed a senior.

SECT. XIX. The visiters for the districts which, or any part of which, be southward and westward of James river, as known by that name, or by the names of Fluvanna and Jackson's river, in every other year, to wit, at the probation meetings held in the years, distinguished in the Christian computation by odd numbers, and the visiters for all the other districts at their said meetings to be held in those years, distinguished by even numbers, after diligent examination and enquiry as before directed, shall chuse one among the said seniors, of the best learning and most helpful genius and disposition, who shall be authorized by them to proceed to William and Mary College; there to be educated, boarded, and clothed, three years; the expence of which annually shall be paid by the Treasurer on warrant from the Auditors.

Appendixes

APPENDIX II

EXTRACTS FROM "NOTES ON THE STATE OF VIRGINIA,"
QUERIES XIV AND XV, 1781–1785

(Padover, pp. 667–670)

CONCLUDING PARAGRAPHS OF QUERY XIV, ENTITLED "THE ADMINISTRATION
OF JUSTICE AND THE DESCRIPTION OF THE LAWS"

Another object of the revisal is, to diffuse knowledge more generally through the mass of the people. This bill proposes to lay off every county into small districts of five or six miles square, called hundreds, and in each of them to establish a school for teaching reading, writing, and arithmetic. The tutor to be supported by the hundred, and every person in it entitled to send their children three years gratis, and as much longer as they please, paying for it. These schools to be under a visitor who is annually to choose the boy of best genius in the school, of those whose parents are too poor to give them further education, and to send him forward to one of the grammar schools, of which twenty are proposed to be erected in different parts of the country, for teaching Greek, Latin, Geography, and the higher branches of numerical arithmetic. Of the boys thus sent in one year, trial is to be made at the grammar schools one or two years, and the best genius of the whole selected, and continued six years, and the residue dismissed. By this means twenty of the best geniuses will be raked from the rubbish annually, and be instructed, at the public expense, so far as the grammar schools go. At the end of six years' instruction, one half are to be discontinued (from among whom the grammar schools will probably be supplied with future masters); and the other half, who are to be chosen for the superiority of their parts and disposition, are to be sent and continued three years in the study of such sciences as they shall choose, at William and Mary college, the plan of which is proposed to be enlarged, as will be hereafter explained, and extended to all the useful sciences. The ultimate result of the whole scheme of education would be the teaching all the children of the State reading, writing, and common arithmetic; turning out ten annually, of superior genius, well taught in Greek, Latin, Geography, and the higher branches of arithmetic; turning out ten others annually, of still superior parts, who, to those branches of learning, shall have added such of the sciences as their genius shall have led them to; the furnishing of the wealthier part of the people convenient schools at which their children may be educated at their own expense. The general objects of this law are to provide an education adapted to the years, to the capacity, and the condition of everyone, and directed to their freedom and happiness. Specific details were not proper for the law. These must be the business of the visitors entrusted with its execution. The first stage of this education being the schools of the hundreds, wherein the great mass of the people will receive their instruction, the principal foundations of future order will be laid here. Instead, therefore, of putting the Bible and Testament into the hands of the children at an age when their judgments are not sufficiently matured for religious inquiries, their memories may here be stored with the most useful facts from Grecian, Roman, European and American history. The first elements of morality too may be instilled into their minds; such as, when further developed as their judgments advance in strength, may teach them how to work out their own greatest happiness, by showing them that it does not depend on the condition of life in which chance has placed them, but is always the result of a good conscience, good health, occupation, and freedom in all just pursuits. Those whom either the wealth of their parents or the adoption of the State shall destine to higher degrees of learning, will go on to the grammar schools, which constitute the next stage, there to be instructed in the languages. The learning Greek and Latin, I am told, is going into disuse in Europe. I know not what their manners and occupations may call for; but it would be very ill-judged in us to follow their example in this instance. There is a certain period of life, say from eight to fifteen or sixteen years of age, when the mind like the body is not yet firm enough for laborious and close operations. If applied to such, it falls an early victim to premature exertion; exhibiting, indeed, at first, in these young and tender subjects, the flattering appearance of their being men while they are yet children, but ending in reducing them to be children when they should be men. The memory is then most susceptible and tenacious of impressions; and the learning of languages being chiefly a work of memory, it seems precisely fitted to the powers of this period, which is long enough too for acquiring the most useful languages, ancient and modern. I do not pretend that language is science. It is only an instrument for the attainment of science. But that time is not lost which is employed in providing tools for future operation; more especially as in this case the books put into the hands of the youth for this purpose may be such as will at the same time impress their minds with useful facts and good principles. If this period be suffered to pass in idleness, the mind becomes lethargic and impotent, as would the body it inhabits if unexercised during the same time. The sympathy between body and mind during their rise, progress and decline, is too strict and obvious to endanger our being missed while we reason from the one to the other. As soon as they are of sufficient age, it is supposed they will be sent on from the grammar schools to the university, which constitutes our third and last stage, there to study those sciences which may be adapted to their views. By that part of our plan which prescribes the selection of the youths of genius from among the classes of the poor, we hope to avail the State of those talents which nature has sown as liberally among the poor as the rich, but which perish without use, if not sought for and cultivated. But of the views of this law none is more important, none more legitimate, than that of rendering the people the safe, as they are the ultimate, guardians of their own liberty. For this purpose the reading in the first stage, where *they* will receive their whole education, is proposed, as has been said, to be chiefly historical. History, by apprizing them of the past, will enable them to judge of the future; it will avail them of the experience of other times and other nations; it will qualify them as judges of the actions and designs of men; it will enable them to know ambition under every disguise it may assume; and knowing it, to defeat its views. In every government on earth is some trace of human weakness, some germ of corruption and degeneracy, which cunning will discover, and wickedness insensibly open, cultivate and improve. Every government degenerates when trusted to the rulers of the people alone. The people themselves therefore are its only safe depositories. And to render even them safe, their minds must be improved to a certain degree. This indeed is not all that is necessary, though it be essentially necessary. An amendment of our constitution must here come in aid of the public education. The influence over government must be shared among all the people. If every individual which composes their mass participates of the ultimate authority, the government will be safe; because the corrupting the whole mass will exceed any private resources of wealth; and public ones cannot be provided but by levies on the people. In this case every man would have to pay his own price. The government of Great Britain has been corrupted, because but one man in ten has a right to vote for members of parliament. The sellers of the government, therefore, get nine-tenths of their price clear. It has been thought that corruption is restrained by confining the right of suffrage to a few of the wealthier of the people; but it would be more effectually restrained by an extension of that right to such numbers as would bid defiance to the means of corruption.

QUERY XV

The Colleges and Public Establishments, the Roads, Buildings, &c.

The college of William and Mary is the only public seminary of learning in this State. It was founded in the time of king William and queen Mary, who granted to it twenty thousand acres of land, and a penny a pound duty on certain tobaccoes exported from Virginia and Maryland, which had been levied by the statute of 25 Car. II. The assembly also gave it, by temporary laws, a duty on liquors imported, and skins and furs exported. From these resources it received upwards of three thousand pounds *communibus annis*. The buildings are of brick, sufficient for an indifferent accommodation of perhaps an hundred students. By its charter it was to be under the government of twenty visitors, who were to be its legislators, and to have a president and six professors, who were incorporated. It was allowed a representative in the general assembly. Under this charter, a professorship of the Greek and Latin languages, a professorship of mathematics, one of moral philosophy, and two of divinity, were established. To these were annexed, for a sixth professorship, a considerable donation by Mr. Boyle, of England, for the instruction of the Indians, and their conversion to Christianity. This was called the professorship of Brafferton, from an estate of that name in England, purchased with the monies given. The admission of the learners of Latin and Greek filled the college with children. This rendering it disagreeable and degrading to young gentlemen already prepared for entering on the sciences, they were discouraged from resorting to it, and thus the schools for mathematics and moral philosophy, which might have been of some service, became of very little. The revenues, too, were exhausted in accommodating those who came only to acquire the rudiments of science. After the present revolution, the visitors, having no power to change those circumstances in the constitution of the college which were fixed by the charter, and being therefore confined in the number of the professorships, undertook to change the objects of the professorships. They excluded the two schools for divinity, and that for the Greek and Latin languages, and substituted others; so that at present they stand thus:

A Professorship for Law and Police;
    Anatomy and Medicine;
    Natural Philosophy and Mathematics;
    Moral Philosophy, the Law of Nature and Nations, the Fine Arts;
    Modern Languages;
    For the Brafferton.

And it is proposed, so soon as the legislature shall have leisure to take up this subject, to desire authority from them to increase the number of professorships, as well for the purpose of subdividing those already instituted, as of adding others for other branches of science. To the professorships usually established in the universities of Europe, it would seem proper to add one for the ancient languages and literature of the north, on account of their connection with our own language, laws, customs, and history. The purposes of the Brafferton institution would be better answered by maintaining a perpetual mission among the Indian tribes, the object of which, besides instructing them in the principles of Christianity, as the founder requires, should be to collect their traditions, laws, customs, languages, and other circumstances which might lead to a discovery of their relation with one another, or descent from other nations. When these objects are accomplished with one tribe, the missionary might pass on to another.

APPENDIX III

EXTRACT FROM A LETTER TO GEORGE WASHINGTON
FROM PARIS, JANUARY 4 [1786]
(Boyd, vol. IX, p. 150)

The institutions you propose to establish by the shares in the Patowmac and James river companies given you by the assembly, and the particular objects of those institutions are most worthy. It occurs to me however that if the bill 'for the more general diffusion of knowledge' which is in the revisal, should be passed, it would supersede the use, and obscure the existence of the charity schools you have thought of. I suppose in fact that that bill, or some other like it, would be passed. I never saw one received with more enthusiasm than that was by the house of delegates in the year 1778, and ordered to be printed, and it seemed afterwards that nothing but the extreme distress of our resources prevented it's being carried into execution even during the war. It is an axiom in my mind that our liberty can never be safe but in the hands of the people themselves, and that too of the people with a certain degree of instruction. This it is the business of the state to effect, and on a general plan. Should you see a probability of this however, you can never be at a loss for worthy objects of this donation. Even the remitting that proportion of the toll on all articles transported would present itself under many favorable considerations, and it would in effect be to make the state do in a certain proportion what they ought to have done wholly; for I think they should clear all the rivers and lay them open and free to all. However you are infinitely the best judge how the most good may be effected with these shares.

All is quiet here. There are indeed two specks in the horizon, the exchange of Bavaria, and the demarcation between the Emperor and Turks. We may add as a third the interference by the king of Prussia in the domestic disputes of the Dutch. Great Britain, it is said, begins to look towards us with a little more good humour. But how true this may be I cannot say with certainty. We are trying to render her commerce as little necessary to us as possible by finding other markets for our produce. A most favourable reduction of duties on whale oil has taken place here, which will give us a vent for that article paying a duty of a guinea and a half a ton only.

I have the honor to be with the highest esteem & respect Dear Sir Your most obedient and most humble servant,

TH: JEFFERSON

APPENDIX IV

EXTRACT FROM A LETTER TO GEORGE WYTHE
FROM PARIS, AUGUST 13, 1786
(Boyd vol. X, p. 245)

The European papers have announced that the assembly of Virginia were occupied on the revisal of their Code of laws. This, with some other similar intelligence, has contributed much to convince the people of Europe, that what the English papers are constantly publishing of our anarchy, is false; as they are sensible that such a work is that of a people only who are in perfect tranquillity. Our act for freedom of religion is extremely applauded. The Ambassadors and ministers of the several nations of Europe resident at this court have asked of me copies of it to send to their sovereigns, and it is inserted at full length in several books now in the press; among others, in the new Encyclopedie. I think it will produce considerable good even in these countries where ignorance, superstition, poverty and oppression of body and mind in every form, are so firmly settled on the mass of the people, that their redemption from them can never be hoped. If the almighty had begotten a thousand sons, instead of one, they would not have sufficed for this task. If all the sovereigns of Europe were to set themselves to work to emancipate the minds of their subjects from their present ignorance and prejudices, and that as zealously as they now endeavor the contrary, a thousand years would not place them on that high ground on which our common people are now setting out. Ours could not have been so fairly put into the hands of their own common sense, had they not been separated from their parent stock and been kept from contamination, either from them, or the other people of the old world, by the intervention of so wide an ocean. To know the worth of this, one must see the want of it here. I think by far the most important bill in our whole code is that for the diffusion of knowledge among the people. No other sure foundation can be devised for the preservation of freedom, and happiness. If any body thinks that kings, nobles, or priests are good conservators of the public happiness,* send them here. It is the best school in the universe to cure them of that folly. They will see here with their own eyes that these descriptions of men are an abandoned confederacy against the happiness of the mass of people. The omnipotence of their effect cannot be better proved than in this country particularly, where notwithstanding the finest soil upon earth, the finest climate under heaven, and a people of the most benevolent, the most gay, and amiable character of which the human form is susceptible, where such a people I say, surrounded by so many blessings from nature, are yet loaded with misery by kings, nobles and priests, and by them alone. Preach, my dear Sir, a crusade against ignorance; establish and improve the law for educating the common people. Let our countrymen know that the people alone can protect us against these evils, and that the tax which will be paid for this purpose is not more than the thousandth part of what will be paid to kings, priests and nobles who will rise up among us if we leave the people in ignorance.—The people of England, I think, are less oppressed than here. But it needs but half an eye to see, when among them, that the foundation is laid in their dispositions, for the establishment of a despotism. Nobility, wealth, and pomp are the objects of their adoration. They are by no means the free-minded people we suppose them in America. Their learned men too are few in number, and are less learned and infinitely less emancipated from prejudice than those of this country. An event too seems to be prospering, in the order of things, which will probably decide the fate of that country. It is no longer doubtful that the harbour of Cherbourg will be completed, that it will be a most excellent one, and capacious enough to hold the whole navy of France. Nothing has ever been wanting to enable this country to invade that, but a naval force conveniently stationed to protect the transports. This change of situation, must oblige the English to keep up a great standing army, and there is no king, who, with a sufficient

---

* The preceding seven words were interlined in substitution for: "could give any aid towards their preservation," deleted [Boyd's note].

force, is not always ready to make himself absolute.—My paper warns me it is time to recommend myself to the friendly recollection of Mrs. Wythe, of Colo. Taliaferro and his family and particularly of Mr. R. T. and to assure you of the affectionate esteem with which I am Dear Sir your friend & servt.,

TH: JEFFERSON

APPENDIX V

LETTER TO JEFFERSON'S NEPHEW, PETER CARR, FROM PARIS, AUGUST 10, 1787

(Padover, pp. 1057–1060)

DEAR PETER: I have received your two letters of December the 30th and April the 18th, and am very happy to find by them, as well as by letters from Mr. Wythe, that you have been so fortunate as to attract his notice and good will; I am sure you will find this to have been one of the most fortunate events of your life, as I have ever been sensible it was of mine. I enclose you a sketch of the sciences to which I would wish you to apply, in such order as Mr. Wythe shall advise; I mention, also, the books in them worth your reading, which submit to his correction. Many of these are among your father's books, which you should have brought to you. As I do not recollect those of them not in his library, you must write to me for them, making out a catalogue of such as you think you shall have occasion for, in eighteen months from the date of your letter, and consulting Mr. Wythe on the subject. To this sketch, I will add a few particular observations:

1. Italian. I fear the learning this language will confound your French and Spanish. Being all of them degenerated dialects of the Latin, they are apt to mix in conversation. I have never seen a person speaking the three languages, who did not mix them. It is a delightful language, but late events having rendered the Spanish more useful, lay it aside to prosecute that.

2. Spanish. Bestow great attention on this, and endeavor to acquire an accurate knowledge of it. Our future connections with Spain and Spanish America, will render that language a valuable acquisition. The ancient history of that part of America, too, is written in that language. I send you a dictionary.

3. Moral Philosophy. I think it lost time to attend lectures on this branch. He who made us would have been a pitiful bungler, if he had made the rules of our moral conduct a matter of science. For one man of science, there are thousands who are not. What would have become of them? Man was destined for society. His morality, therefore, was to be formed to this object. He was endowed with a sense of right and wrong, merely relative to this. This sense is as much a part of his nature, as the sense of hearing, seeing, feeling; it is the true foundation of morality, and not the το χαλον,

100

truth, &c., as fanciful writers have imagined. The moral sense, or conscience, is as much a part of man as his leg or arm. It is given to all human beings in a stronger or weaker degree, as force of members is given them in a greater or less degree. It may be strengthened by exercise, as may any particular limb of the body. This sense is submitted, indeed, in some degree, to the guidance of reason; but it is a small stock which is required for this: even a less one than what we call common sense. State a moral case to a plough-man and a professor. The former will decide it as well, and often better than the latter, because he has not been led astray by artificial rules. In this branch therefore, read good books, because they will encourage, as well as direct your feelings. The writings of Sterne, particularly, form the best course of morality that ever was written. Besides these, read the books mentioned in the enclosed paper; and, above all things, lose no occasion of exercising your dispositions to be grateful, to be generous, to be charitable, to be humane, to be true, just, firm, orderly, courageous, &c. Consider every act of this kind, as an exercise which will strengthen your moral faculties and increase your worth.

4. Religion. Your reason is now mature enough to examine this object. In the first place, divest yourself of all bias in favor of novelty and singularity of opinion. Indulge them in any other subject rather than that of religion. It is too important, and the consequences of error may be too serious. On the other hand, shake off all the fears and servile prejudices, under which weak minds are servilely crouched. Fix reason firmly in her seat, and call to her tribunal every fact, every opinion. Question with boldness even the existence of a God; because, if there be one, he must more approve of the homage of reason, than that of blindfolded fear. You will naturally examine first, the religion of your own country. Read the Bible, then, as you would read Livy or Tacitus. The facts which are within the ordinary course of nature, you will believe on the authority of the writer, as you do those of the same kind in Livy and Tacitus. The testimony of the writer weighs in their favor, in one scale, and their not being against the laws of nature, does not weigh against them. But those facts in the Bible which contradict the laws of nature, must be examined with more care, and under a variety of faces. Here you must recur to the pretensions of the writer to inspiration from God. Examine upon what evidence his pretensions are founded, and whether that evidence is so strong, as that its falsehood would be more improbable than a change in the laws of nature, in the case he relates. For example, in the book of Joshua, we are told, the sun stood still several hours. Were we to read that fact in Livy or Tacitus, we should class it with their showers of blood, speaking of statues, beasts, &c. But it is said, that the writer of that book was inspired. Examine, therefore, candidly, what evidence there is of his having been inspired. The pretension is entitled to your inquiry, because millions believe it. On the other hand, you are astronomer enough to know how contrary it is to the law of nature that a body revolving on its axis, as the earth does, should have stopped, should not, by that sudden stoppage, have prostrated animals, trees, buildings, and should after a certain time have resumed its revolution, and that without a second general prostration. Is this arrest of the earth's motion, or the evi-

dence which affirms it, most within the law of probabilities? You will next read the New Testament. It is the history of a personage called Jesus. Keep in your eye the opposite pretensions: 1, of those who say he was begotten by God, born of a virgin, suspended and reversed the laws of nature at will, and ascended bodily into heaven; and 2, of those who say he was a man of illegitimate birth, of a benevolent heart, enthusiastic mind, who set out without pretensions to divinity, ended in believing them, and was punished capitally for sedition, by being gibbeted, according to the Roman law, which punished the first commission of that offence by whipping, and the second by exile, or death *in furea*. See this law in the Digest, Lib. 98. tit. 19. § 28. 3. and Lipsius Lib. 2. de cruce. cap. 2. These questions are examined in the books I have mentioned, under the head of Religion, and several others. They will assist you in your inquiries; but keep your reason firmly on the watch in reading them all. Do not be frightened from this inquiry by any fear of its consequences. If it ends in a belief that there is no God, you will find incitements to virtue in the comfort and pleasantness you feel in its exercise, and the love of others which it will procure you. If you find reason to believe there is a God, a consciousness that you are acting under his eye, and that he approves you, will be a vast additional incitement; if that there be a future state, the hope of a happy existence in that increases the appetite to deserve it; if that Jesus was also a God, you will be comforted by a belief of his aid and love. In fine, I repeat, you must lay aside all prejudice on both sides, and neither believe nor reject anything, because any other persons, or description of persons, have rejected or believed it. Your own reason is the only oracle given you by heaven, and you are answerable, not for the rightness, but uprightness of the decision. I forgot to observe, when speaking of the New Testament, that you should read all the histories of Christ, as well of those whom a council of ecclesiastics have decided for us to be Pseudo-evangelists, as those they named Evangelists. Because these Pseudo-evangelists pretended to inspiration, as much as the others, and you are to judge their pretensions by your own reason, and not by the reason of those ecclesiastics. Most of these are lost. There are some, however, still extant, collected by Fabricius, which I will endeavor to get and send you.

5. Travelling. This makes men wiser, but less happy. When men of sober age travel, they gather knowledge, which they may apply usefully for their country; but they are subject ever after to recollections mixed with regret; their affections are weakened by being extended over more objects; and they learn new habits which cannot be gratified when they return home. Young men, who travel, are exposed to all these inconveniences in a higher degree, to others still more serious, and do not acquire that wisdom for which a previous foundation is requisite, by repeated and just observations at home. The glare of pomp and pleasure is analogous to the motion of the blood; it absorbs all their affection and attention, they are torn from it as from the only good in this world, and return to their home as to a place of exile and condemnation. Their eyes are forever turned back to the object they have lost, and its recollection poisons the residue of their lives. Their first and most delicate passions are hackneyed on unworthy objects

here, and they carry home the dregs, insufficient to make themselves or anybody else happy. Add to this, that a habit of idleness, an inability to apply themselves to business is acquired, and renders them useless to themselves and their country. These observations are founded in experience. There is no place where your pursuit of knowledge will be so little obstructed by foreign objects, as in your own country, nor any, wherein the virtues of the heart will be less exposed to be weakened. Be good, be learned, and be industrious, and you will not want the aid of travelling, to render you precious to your country, dear to your friends, happy within yourself. I repeat my advice, to take a great deal of exercise, and on foot. Health is the first requisite after morality. Write to me often, and be assured of the interest I take in your success, as well as the warmth of those sentiments of attachment with which I am, dear Peter, your affectionate friend.

APPENDIX VI

EXTRACT FROM A LETTER TO JOSEPH PRIESTLEY
FROM PHILADELPHIA, JANUARY 18, 1800
(Honeywell, Appendix C, pp. 215–216)

We have in that State a College (William and Mary) just well enough endowed to draw out the miserable existence to which a miserable constitution has doomed it. It is moreover eccentric in its position, exposed to all bilious diseases as all the lower country is, and therefore abandoned by the public care, as that part of the country itself is in a considerable degree by its inhabitants. We wish to establish in the upper country, and more centrally for the State, an University on a plan so broad and liberal and *modern*, as to be worth patronizing with the public support, and be a temptation to the youth of other States to come and drink of the cup of knowledge and fraternize with us. The first step is to obtain a good plan; that is, a judicious selection of the sciences, and a practicable grouping of some of them together, and ramifying of others, so as to adapt the professorships to our uses and our means. In an institution meant chiefly for use, some branches of science, formerly esteemed, may be now omitted; so may others now valued in Europe, but useless to us for ages to come. As an example of the former, the Oriental learning, and of the latter, almost the whole of the institution proposed to Congress by the Secretary of War's report of the 5th instant. Now there is no one to whom this subject is so familiar as yourself. There is no one in the world who, equally with yourself, unites this full possession of the subject with such a knowledge of the state of our existence, as enables you to fit the garment to him who is to *pay* for and to *wear* it. To you therefore we address our solicitations, and to lessen to you as much as possible the ambiguities of our object, I will venture even to sketch the sciences which seem useful and practicable for us, as they occur to me while holding my pen. Botany, chemistry, zoölogy, anatomy, surgery, medicine, natural philosophy, agriculture, mathematics, astronomy, geography, politics, commerce, history, ethics, law, arts, fine arts. This list is imperfect because I make it hastily, and because I am unequal to the subject. It is evident that some of these articles are too much for one professor and must therefore be ramified; others may be ascribed in groups to a single professor. This is the difficult part of the work, and requires a head perfectly knowing the extent of each branch, and the limits within which it may be circumscribed, so as to bring the whole within the powers of the fewest professors possible, and consequently within the degree of expense practicable for us. We should propose that the professors follow no other calling, so that their whole time may be given to their academical functions; and we should propose to draw from Europe the first characters in science, by considerable temptations, which would not need to be repeated after the first set should have prepared fit successors and given reputation to the institution. From some splendid characters I have received offers most perfectly reasonable and practicable.

I do not propose to give you all this trouble merely of my own head, that would be arrogance. It has been the subject of consultation among the ablest and highest characters of our State, who only wait for a plan to make a joint and I hope a successful effort to get the thing carried into effect. They will receive your ideas with the greatest deference and thankfulness. We shall be here certainly for two months to come; but should you not have leisure to think of it before Congress adjourns, it will come safely to me afterwards by post, the nearest post office being Milton.

APPENDIX VII

EXTRACT FROM A LETTER TO PICTET
FROM WASHINGTON, D.C., FEBRUARY 5, 1803

(Lipscomb, vol. X, pp. 355–357)

DEAR SIR,—It is long since I might have acknowledged your favor of May 20, 1801, which, however, I did not receive till January, 1802. My incessant occupations on matters which will not bear delay, occasion those which can be put off to lie often for a considerable time. I rejoice that the opinion which I gave you on the removal hither proved useful. I knew it was not safe for you to take such a step until it would be done on sure ground. I hoped at that time that some canal shares, which were at the disposal of General Washington, might have been applied towards the establishment of a good seminary of learning; but he had already proceeded too far on another plan to change their direction. I have still had constantly in view to propose to the legislature of Virginia the establishment of one on as large a scale as our present circumstances would require or bear. But as yet no favorable moment has occurred. In the meanwhile I am endeavoring to procure materials for a good plan. With this view I am to ask the favor of you to give me a sketch of the branches of science taught in your college, how they are distributed among the professors, that is to say, how many professors there are, and what branches of science are allotted to each professor, and the days and hours assigned to each branch. Your successful experience in the distribution of business will be a valuable guide to us, who are without experience. I am sensible I am imposing on your goodness a troublesome task; but I believe every son of science feels a strong and disinterested desire of promoting it in every part of the earth, and it is the consciousness as well as confidence in this which emboldens me to make the present request.

In the line of science we have little new here. Our citizens almost all follow some industrious occupation, and, therefore, have little time to devote to abstract science. In the arts, and especially in the mechanical arts, many ingenious improvements are made in consequence of the patent-right giving exclusive use of them for fourteen years. But the great mass of our people are agricultural; and the commercial cities, though, by the command of newspapers, they make a great deal of noise, have little effect in the direction of the government. They are as different in sentiment and character from the country people as any two distinct nations, and are clamorous against the order of things established by the agricultural interest. Under this order, our citizens generally are enjoying a very great degree of liberty and security in the most temperate manner. Every man being at his ease, feels an interest in the preservation of order, and comes forth to preserve it at the first call of the magistrate. We are endeavoring, too, to reduce the government to the practice of a rigorous economy, to avoid burdening the people, and arming the magistrate with a patronage of money, which might be used to corrupt and undermine the principles of our government. I state these general outlines to you, because I believe you take some interest in our fortune, and because our newspapers, for the most part, present only the caricatures of disaffected minds. Indeed, the abuses of the freedom of the press here have been carried to a length never before known or borne by any civilized nation. But it is so difficult to draw a clear line of separation between the abuse and the wholesome use of the press, that as yet we have found it better to trust the public judgment, rather than the magistrate, with the discrimination between truth and falsehood. And hitherto the public judgment has performed that office with wonderful correctness. Should you favor me with a letter, the safest channel of conveyance will be the American minister at Paris or London. I pray you to accept assurances of my great esteem, and high respect and consideration.

Appendixes

APPENDIX VIII

EXTRACT FROM PRESIDENT JEFFERSON'S SIXTH ANNUAL MESSAGE,
DECEMBER 2, 1806

(Padover, pp. 421–426)

The duties composing the Mediterranean fund will cease by law at the end of the present season. Considering, however, that they are levied chiefly on luxuries, and that we have an impost on salt, a necessary of life, the free use of which otherwise is so important, I recommend to your consideration the suppression of the duties on salt, and the continuation of the Mediterranean fund, instead thereof, for a short time, after which that also will become unnecessary for any purpose now within contemplation.

When both of these branches of revenue shall in this way be relinquished, there will still ere long be an accumulation of moneys in the treasury beyond the instalments of public debt which we are permitted by contract to pay. They cannot, then, without a modification assented to by the public creditors, be applied to the extinguishment of this debt, and the complete liberation of our revenues—the most desirable of all objects; nor, if our peace continues, will they be wanting for any other existing purpose. The question, therefore, now comes forward,—to what other objects shall these surpluses be appropriated, and the whole surplus of impost, after the entire discharge of the public debt, and during those intervals when the purposes of war shall not call for them? Shall we suppress the impost and give that advantage to foreign over domestic manufactures? On a few articles of more general and necessary use, the suppression in due season will doubtless be right, but the great mass of the articles on which impost is paid is foreign luxuries, purchased by those only who are rich enough to afford themselves the use of them. Their patriotism would certainly prefer its continuance and application to the great purposes of the public education, roads, rivers, canals, and such other objects of public improvement as it may be thought proper to add to the constitutional enumeration of federal powers. By these operations new channels of communication will be opened between the States; the lines of separation will disappear, their interests will be identified, and their union cemented by new and indissoluble ties. Education is here placed among the articles of public care, not that it would be proposed to take its ordinary branches out of the hands of private enterprise, which manages so much better all the concerns to which it is equal; but a public institution can alone supply those sciences which, though rarely called for, are yet necessary to complete the circle, all the parts of which contribute to the improvement of the country, and some of them to its preservation. The subject is now proposed for the consideration of Congress, because, if approved by the time the State legislatures shall have deliberated on this extension of the federal trusts, and the laws shall be passed, and other arrangements made for their execution, the necessary funds will be on hand and without employment. I suppose an amendment to the constitution, by consent of the States, necessary, because the objects now recommended are not among those enumerated in the constitution, and to which it permits the public moneys to be applied.

The present consideration of a national establishment for education, particularly, is rendered proper by this circumstance also, that if Congress, approving the proposition, shall yet think it more eligible to found it on a donation of lands, they have it now in their power to endow it with those which will be among the earliest to produce the necessary income. This foundation would have the advantage of being independent on war, which may suspend other improvements by requiring for its own purposes the resources destined for them.

APPENDIX IX

EXTRACT FROM A LETTER TO JOHN ADAMS
FROM MONTICELLO, OCTOBER 28, 1813

(Lester J. Cappon, ed., *Adams-Jefferson Letters* [Chapel Hill, N.C.: University of North Carolina Press, 1959], vol. II, pp. 387–392)

DEAR SIR

According to the reservation between us, of taking up one of the subjects of our correspondence at a time, I turn to your letter of Aug. 16. and Sep. 2.

The passage you quote from Theognis, I think has an Ethical, rather than a political object. The whole piece is a moral *exhortation, παραίνεσις,* and this passage particularly seems to be a reproof to man, who, while with his domestic animals he is curious to improve the race by employing always the finest male, pays no attention to the improvement of his own race, but intermarries with the vicious, the ugly, or the old, for considerations of wealth or ambition. It is in conformity with the principle adopted afterwards by the Pythagoreans, and expressed by Ocellus in another form. Περι δε τῆς ἐκ τῶν ἀλλήλων ανθρωπων γενεσεως etc.—ουχ ἡδονης ἐνεκα ἡ μιξις. Which, as literally as intelligibility will admit, may be thus translated. 'Concerning the interprocreation of men, how, and of whom it shall be, in a perfect manner, and according to the laws of modesty and sanctity, conjointly, this is what I think right. First to lay it down that we do not commix for the sake of pleasure, but of the procreation of children. For the powers, the organs and desires for coition have not been given by god to man for the sake of pleasure, but for the procreation of the race. For as it were incongruous for a mortal born to partake of divine life, the immortality of the race being taken away, god fulfilled the purpose by making the generations uninterrupted and continuous. This therefore we are especially to lay down as a principle, that coition is not for the sake of pleasure.' But Nature, not trusting to this moral and abstract motive, seems to have provided more securely for the perpetuation of the species by making it the effect of the oestrum implant in the constitution of both sexes. And not only has the commerce of love been indulged on this unhallowed impulse, but made subservient also to wealth and ambition by marriages without regard to the beauty, the healthiness, the understanding, or virtue of the subject from which we are to breed. The selecting the best male for a Haram of well chosen females also, which Theognis seems to recommend from the example of our sheep and asses, would doubtless improve the human, as it does the brute animal, and produce a race of veritable αριστοι ["aristocrats"]. For experience proves that the moral and physical qualities of man, whether good or evil, are transmissible in a certain degree from father to son. But I suspect that the equal rights of men will rise up against this privileged Solomon, and oblige us to continue acquiescence under the 'Αμαυρωσις γενεος αστων ["the degeneration of the race of men"] which Theognis complains of, and to content ourselves with the accidental aristoi produced by the fortuitous concourse of breeders. For I agree with you that there is a natural aristocracy among men. The grounds of this are virtue and talent. Formerly bodily powers gave place among the aristoi. But since the invention of gunpowder has armed the weak as well as the strong with missile death, bodily strength, like beauty, good humor, politeness and other accomplishments, has become but an auxiliary ground of distinction. There is also an artificial aristocracy founded on wealth and birth, without either virtue or talents; for with these it would belong to the first class. The natural aristocracy I consider as the most precious gift of nature for the instruction, the trusts, and government of society. And indeed it would have been inconsistent in creation to have formed man for the social state, and not to have provided virtue and wisdom enough to manage the concerns of the society. May we not even say that that form of government is the best which provides the most effectually for a pure selection of these natural aristoi into the offices of government? The artificial aristocracy is a mischievous ingredient in government, and provision should be made to prevent it's ascendancy. On the question, What is the best provision, you and I differ; but we differ as rational friends, using the free exercise of our own reason, and mutually indulging it's errors. *You* think it best to put the Pseudo-aristoi into a separate chamber of legislation where they may be hindered from doing mischief by their coordinate branches, and where also they may be a protection to wealth against the Agrarian and plundering enterprises of the Majority of the people. I think that to give them power in order to prevent them from doing mischief, is arming them for it, and increasing instead of remedying the evil. For if the coordinate branches can arrest their action, so may they that of the coordinates. Mischief may be done negatively as well as positively. Of this a cabal in the Senate of the U. S. has furnished many proofs. Nor do I believe them necessary to protect the wealthy; because enough of these will find their way into every branch of the legislation to protect themselves. From 15. to 20. legislatures of our own, in action for 30. years past, have proved that no fears of an equalisation of property are to be apprehended from them.

I think the best remedy is exactly that provided by all our constitutions, to leave to the citizens the free election and separation of the aristoi from the pseudo-aristoi, of the wheat from the chaff. In general they will elect the real good and wise. In some instances, wealthy may corrupt, and birth blind them, but not in sufficient degree to endanger the society.

It is probable that our difference of opinion may in some measure be produced by a difference of character in those among whom we live. From what I have seen of Massachusets and Connecticut myself, and still more from what I have heard, and the character given of the former by yourself, who know them so much better, there seems to be in those two states a traditionary reverence for certain families, which has rendered the offices of the government nearly hereditary in those families. I presume that from an early period of your history, members of these families happening to possess virtue and talents, have honestly exercised them for the good of the people, and by their services have endeared their names to them.

In coupling Connecticut with you, I mean it politically only, not morally. For having made the Bible the Common law of their land they seem to have modelled their morality on the story of Jacob and Laban. But altho' this hereditary succession to office with you may in some degree be founded in real family merit, yet in a much higher degree it has proceeded from your strict alliance of church and state. These families are canonised in the eyes of the people on the common principle 'you tickle me, and I will tickle you.' In Virginia we have nothing of this. Our clergy, before the revolution, having been secured against rivalship by fixed salaries, did not give themselves the trouble of acquiring influence over the people. Of wealth, there were great accumulations in particular families, handed down from generation to generation under the English law of entails. But the only object of ambition for the wealthy was a seat in the king's council. All their court then was paid to the crown and it's creatures; and they Philipised in all collisions between the king and people. Hence they were unpopular; and that unpopularity continues attached to their names. A Randolph, a Carter, or a Burwell must have great personal superiority over a common competitor to be elected by the people, even at this day.

At the first session of our legislature after the Declaration of Independance, we passed a law abolishing entails. And this was followed by one abolishing the privilege of Primogeniture, and dividing the lands of intestates equally among all their children, or other representatives. These laws, drawn by myself, laid the axe to the root of Pseudo-aristocracy. And had another which I prepared been adopted by the legislature, our work would have been compleat. It was a Bill for the more general diffusion of learning. This proposed to divide every country into wards of 5. or 6. miles square, like your townships; to establish in each ward a free school for reading, writing and common arithmetic; to provide for the annual selection of the best subjects from these schools who might receive at the public expence a higher degree of education at a district school; and from these district schools to select a certain number of the most promising subjects to be compleated at an University, where all the useful sciences should be taught. Worth and genius would thus have been sought out from every condition of life, and compleately prepared by education for defeating the competition of wealth and birth for public trusts.

My proposition had for a further object to impart to these wards those portions of self-government for which they are best qualified, by confiding to them the care of their poor, their roads, police, elections, the nomination of jurors, administration of justice in small cases, elementary exercises of militia, in short, to have made them little republics, with a Warden at the head of each, for all those concerns which, being under their eye, they would better manage than the larger republics of the country or state. A general call of ward-meetings by their Wardens on the same day thro' the state would at any time produce the genuine sense of the people on any required point, and would enable the state to act in mass, as your people have so often done, and with so much effect, by their town meetings. The law for religious freedom, which made a part of this system, having put down the aristocracy of the clergy, and restored to the citizen the freedom of the mind, and those of entails and descents nurturing an equality of condition among them, this on Education would have raised the mass of the people to the high ground of moral respectability necessary to their own safety, and to orderly government; and would have compleated the great object of qualifying them to select the veritable aristoi, for the trusts of government, to the exclusion of the Pseuda-lists: and the same Theognis who has furnished the epigraphs of your two letters assures us that 'ουδεμιαν πω, Κυρν' αγαθοι πολιν ωλεσαν ανδρες ["Curnis, good men have never harmed any city"].' Altho' this law has not yet been acted on but in a small and inefficient degree, it is still considered as before the legislature, with other bills of the revised code, not yet taken up, and I have great hope that some patriotic spirit will, at a favorable moment, call it up, and make it the key-stone of the arch of our government.

With respect to Aristocracy, we should further consider that, before the establishment of the American states, nothing was known to History but the Man of the old world, crouded within limits either small or overcharged, and steeped in the vices which that situation generates. A government adapted to such men would be one thing; but a very different one that for the Man of these states. Here every one may have land to labor for himself if he chuses; or, preferring the exercise of any other industry, may exact for it such compensation as not only to afford a comfortable subsistence, but wherewith to provide for a cessation from labor in old age. Every one, by his property, or by his satisfactory situation, is interested in the support of law and order. And such men may safely and advantageously reserve to themselves a wholesome controul over their public affairs, and a degree of freedom, which in the hands of the Canaille of the cities of Europe, would be instantly perverted to the demolition and destruction of every thing public and private. The history of the last 25. years of France, and of the last 40. years in America, nay of it's last 200. years, proves the truth of both parts of this observation.

But even in Europe a change has sensibly taken place in the mind of Man. Science had liberated the ideas of those who read and reflect, and the American example had kindled feelings of right in the people. An insurrection has consequently begun, of science, talents and courage against rank and birth, which have fallen into contempt. It has failed in it's first effort, because the mobs of the cities, the instrument used for it's accomplishment, debased by ignorance, poverty and vice, could not be restrained to rational action. But the world will recover from the panic of this first catastrophe. Science is progressive, and talents and enterprize on the alert. Resort may be had to the people of the country, a more governable power from their principles and subordination; and rank, and birth, and tinsel-aristocracy will finally shrink into insignificance, even there. This however we have no right to meddle with. It suffices for us, if the moral and physical condition of our own citizens qualifies them to select the able and good for the direction of their government, with a recurrence of elections at such short periods as will enable them to displace an unfaithful servant before the mischief he meditates may be irremediable.

I have thus stated my opinion on a point on which we differ, not with a view to controversy, for we are both too old to change opinions which are the result of a long life of inquiry and reflection; but on the suggestion of a former letter of yours, that we ought not to die before we have explained ourselves to each other. We acted in perfect harmony thro' a long and perilous contest for our liberty and independance. A constitution has been acquired which, tho' neither of us think perfect, yet both consider as competent to render our fellow-citizens the happiest and the securest on whom the sun has ever shone. If we do not think exactly alike as to it's imperfections, it matters little to our country which, after devoting to it long lives of disinterested labor, we have delivered over to our successors in life, who will be able to take care of it, and of themselves.

APPENDIX X

EXTRACT FROM A LETTER TO THOMAS COOPER, AUGUST 25, 1814

(Lipscomb, vol. XIV, pp. 173–174)

DEAR SIR,—In my letter of January 16th, I mentioned to you that it had long been in contemplation to get an university established in this State, in which all the branches of science useful *to us,* and *at this day,* should be taught in their highest degree, and that this institution should be incorporated with the College and funds of William and Mary. But what are the sciences useful to us, and at this day thought useful to anybody? A glance over Bacon's *arbor scientiae* will show the foundation for this question and how many of his ramifications of science are now lopped off as nugatory. To be prepared for this new establishment, I have taken some pains to ascertain those branches which men of sense, as well as of science, deem worthy of cultivation. To the statements which I have obtained from other sources, I should highly value an addition of one from yourself. You know our country, its pursuits, its faculties, its relations with others, its means of establishing and maintaining an institution of general science, and the spirit of economy with which it requires that these should be administered. Will you then so far contribute to our views as to consider this subject, to make a statement of the branches of science which you think worthy of being taught, as I have before said, at this day, and in this country? But to accommodate them to our economy, it will be necessary further to distribute them into groups, each group comprehending as many branches as one industrious professor may competently teach, and, as much as may be, a duly associated family, or class, of kindred sciences. The object of this is to bring the whole circle of useful science under the direction of the smallest number of professors possible, and that our means may be so frugally employed as to effect the greatest possible good. We are about to make an effort for the introduction of this institution.

APPENDIX XI

LETTER TO PETER CARR, SEPTEMBER 7, 1814, OUTLINING AN EDUCATIONAL PLAN

(Padover, pp. 1064–1069)

DEAR SIR: On the subject of the academy or college proposed to be established in our neighborhood, I promised the trustees that I would prepare for them a plan, adapted, in the first instance, to our slender funds, but susceptible of being enlarged, either by their own growth or by accession from other quarters.

I have long entertained the hope that this, our native State, would take up the subject of education, and make an establishment, either with or without incorporation, into that of William and Mary, where every branch of science, deemed useful at this day, should be taught in its highest degree. With this view, I have lost no occasion of making myself acquainted with the organization of the best seminaries in other countries, and with the opinions of the most enlightened individuals, on the subject of the sciences worthy of a place in such an institution. In order to prepare what I have promised our trustees, I have lately revised these several plans with attention; and I am struck with the diversity of arrangement observable in them—no two alike. Yet, I have no doubt that these several arrangements have been the subject of mature reflection, by wise and learned men, who, contemplating local circumstances, have adapted them to the conditions of the section of society for which they have been framed. I am strengthened in this conclusion by an examination of each separately, and a conviction that no one of them, if adopted without change, would be suited to the circumstances and pursuit of our country. The example they set, then, is authority for us to select from their different institutions the materials which are good for us, and, with them, to erect a structure, whose arrangement shall correspond with our own social condition, and shall admit of enlargement in proportion to the encouragement it may merit and receive. As I may not be able to attend the meetings of the trustees, I will make you the depository of my ideas on the subject, which may be corrected, as you proceed, by the better view of others, and adapted, from time to time, to the prospects which open upon us, and which cannot be specifically seen and provided for.

In the first place, we must ascertain with precision the object of our institution, by taking a survey of the general field of science, and marking out the portion we mean to occupy at first, and the ultimate extension of our views beyond that, should we be enabled to render it, in the end, as comprehensive as we would wish.

1. ELEMENTARY SCHOOLS

It is highly interesting to our country, and it is the duty of its functionaries, to provide that every citizen in it should receive an education proportioned to the condition and pursuits of his life. The mass of our citizens may be divided into two classes—the laboring and the learned. The laboring will need the first grade of education to qualify them for their pursuits and duties; the learned will need it as a foundation for further acquirements. A plan was formerly proposed to the legislature of this State for laying off every county into hundreds or wards of five or six miles square, within each of which should be a school for the education of the children of the ward, wherein they should receive three years' instruction gratis, in reading, writing, arithmetic as far as fractions, the roots and ratios, and geography. The Legislature at one time tried an ineffectual expedient for introducing this plan, which having failed, it is hoped they will some day resume it in a more promising form.

2. GENERAL SCHOOLS

At the discharging of the pupils from the elementary schools, the two classes separate—those destined for labor will engage in the business of agriculture, or enter into apprenticeships to such handicraft art as may be their choice; their companions, destined to the pursuits of science, will proceed to the college, which will consist, 1st of general schools; and 2d, of professional schools. The general schools will constitute the second grade of education.

The learned class may still be subdivided into two sections: 1, Those who are destined for learned professions, as means of livelihood: and 2, The wealthy, who, possessing independent fortunes, may aspire to share in conducting the affairs of the nation, or to live with usefulness and respect in the private ranks of life. Both of these sections will require instruction in all the higher branches of science; the wealthy to qualify them for either public or private life; the professional section will need those branches, especially, which are the basis of their future profession, and a general knowledge of the others, as auxiliary to that, and necessary to their standing and association with the scientific class. All the branches, then, of useful science, ought to be taught in the general schools, to a competent degree, in the first instance. These sciences may be arranged into three departments, not rigorously scientific, indeed, but sufficiently so for our purposes. These are, I. Language II. Mathematics III. Philosophy.

I. Language. In the first department, I would arrange a distinct science: 1, Language and History, ancient and modern; 2, Grammar; 3, Belles Lettres; 4, Rhetoric and Oratory; 5, A school for the deaf, dumb and blind. History is here associated with languages, not as a kindred subject, but on the principle of economy, because both may be attained by the same course of reading, if books are selected with that view.

II. Mathematics. In the department of Mathematics, I should give place distinctly: 1, Mathematics pure; 2, Physico-Mathematics; 3, Physics; 4, Chemistry; 5, Natural History, *to wit:* Mineralogy; 6, Botany; and 7, Zoology; 8, Anatomy; 9, the Theory of Medicine.

III. Philosophy. In the Philosophical department, I should distinguish: 1, Ideology 2, Ethics; 3, the Law of Nature and Nations; 4, Government; 5, Political Economy.

But, some of these terms being used by different writers, in different degrees of extension, I shall define exactly what I mean to comprehend in each of them.

I. 3. Within the term of Belles Lettres I include poetry and composition generally, and criticism.

II. 1. I consider pure mathematics as the science of, 1, Numbers, and 2, Measure in the abstract; that of numbers comprehending Arithmetic, Algebra and Fluxions; that of Measure (under the general appellation of Geometry), comprehending Trigonometry, plane and spherical, conic sections, and transcendental curves.

II. 2. Physico-Mathematics treat of physical subjects by the aid of mathematical calculation. These are Mechanics, Statics, Hydrostatics, Hydrodynamics, Navigation, Astronomy, Geography, Optics, Pneumatics, Acoustics.

II. 3. Physics, or Natural Philosophy (not entering the limits of Chemistry), treat of natural substances, their properties, mutual relations and action. They particularly examine the subjects of motion, action, magnetism, electricity, galvanism, light, meteorology, with an etc. not easily enumerated. These definitions and specifications render immaterial the question whether I use the generic terms in the exact degree of comprehension in which others use them; to be understood is all that is necessary to the present object.

3. PROFESSIONAL SCHOOLS

At the close of this course the students separate; the wealthy retiring, with a sufficient stock of knowledge, to improve themselves to any degree to which their views may lead them, and the professional section to the professional schools, constituting the third grade of education, and teaching the particular sciences which the individuals of this section mean to pursue, with more minuteness and detail than was within the scope of the general schools for the second grade of instruction. In these professional schools each science is to be taught in the highest degree it has yet attained. They are to be the

1st *Department,* the fine arts, to wit: Civil Architecture, Gardening, Painting, Sculpture, and the Theory of Music; the

2d *Department,* Architecture, Military and Naval; Projectiles, Rural Economy (comprehending Agriculture, Horticulture and Veterinary), Technical Philosophy, the Practice of Medicine, Materia Medica, Pharmacy and Surgery. In the

3d *Department,* Theology and Ecclesiastical History; Law, Municipal and Foreign.

To these professional schools will come those who separated at the close of their first elementary course, to wit:

The lawyer to the school of law.

The ecclesiastic to that of theology and ecclesiastical history.

The physician to those of medicine, materia medica, pharmacy and surgery.

The military man to that of military and naval architecture and projectiles.

The agricultor to that of rural economy.

The gentleman, the architect, the pleasure gardener, painter and musician to the school of fine arts.

And to that of technical philosophy will come the mariner, carpenter, shipwright, pumpmaker, clockmaker, machinist, optician, metallurgist, founder, cutler, druggist, brewer, vintner, distiller, dyer, painter, bleacher, soapmaker, tanner, powdermaker, saltmaker, glassmaker, to learn as much as shall be necessary to pursue their art understandingly, of the sciences of geometry, mechanics, statics, hydrostatics, hydraulics, hydrodynamics, navigation, astronomy, geography, optics, pneumatics, physics, chemistry, natural history, botany, mineralogy and pharmacy.

The school of technical philosophy will differ essentially in its functions from the other professional schools. The others are instituted to ramify and dilate the particular sciences taught in the schools of the second grade on a general scale only. The technical school is to abridge those which were taught there too much *in extenso* for the limited wants of the artificer or practical man. These artificers must be grouped together, according to the particular branch of science in which they need elementary and practical instruction; and a special lecture or lectures should be prepared for each group. And these lectures should be given in the evening, so as not to interrupt the labors of the day. The school, particularly, should be maintained wholly at the public expense, on the same principles with that of the ward schools. Through the whole of the collegiate course, at the hours of recreation on certain days, all the students should be taught the manual exercise; military evolutions and manoeuvers should be under a standing organization as a military corps, and with proper officers to train and command them.

A tabular statement of this distribution of the sciences will place the system of instruction more particularly in view:

1st or Elementary Grade in the Ward Schools.

Reading, Writing, Arithmetic, Geography.

2d, or General Grade.

1. Language and History, ancient and modern.
2. Mathematics, *viz.:* Mathematics pure, Physico-Mathematics, Physics, Chemistry, Anatomy, Theory of Medicine, Zoology, Botany and Mineralogy.

3. Philosophy, *viz.*: Ideology, and Ethics, Law of Nature and Nations, Government, Political Economy.

3d, or Professional Grades.

Theology and Ecclesiastical History: Law, Municipal and Foreign; Practice of Medicine; Materia Medica and Pharmacy; Surgery; Architecture, Military and Naval, and Projectiles; Technical Philosophy; Rural Economy; Fine Arts.

On this survey of the field of science, I reccur to the question, what portion of it we mark out for the occupation of our institution? With the first grade of education we shall have nothing to do. The sciences of the second grade are our first object: and, to adapt them to our slender beginnings, we must separate them into groups, comprehending many sciences each, and greatly more, in the first instance, than ought to be imposed on, or can be competently conducted by a single professor permanently. They must be subdivided from time to time, as our means increase, until each professor shall have no more under his care than he can attend to with advantage to his pupils and ease to himself. For the present, we may group the sciences into professorships, as follows, subject, however, to be changed, according to the qualifications of the persons we may be able to engage.

I. Professorship.
Language and History, ancient and modern.
Belles Lettres, Rhetoric and Oratory

II. Professorship.
Mathematics pure, Physico-Mathematics.
Physics, Anatomy, Medicine, Theory

III. Professorship.
Chemistry, Zoology, Botany, Mineralogy.

IV. Professorship.
Philosophy.

APPENDIX XII

EXTRACT FROM A LETTER TO JOSEPH C. CABELL
FROM MONTICELLO, JANUARY 5, 1815

(Cabell, pp. 35–37)

Could the petition which the Albemarle Academy addressed to our Legislature have succeeded at the late session, a little aid additional to the objects of that would have enabled us to have here immediately the best seminary of the United States. I do not know to whom P. Carr (President of the Board of Trustees) committed the petition and papers; but I have seen no trace of their having been offered. Thinking it possible you may not have seen them, I send for your perusal the copies I retained for my own use. They consist— 1. Of a letter to him, sketching, at the request of the trustees, a plan for the institution.* 2. One to Judge Cooper, in answer to some observations he had favored me with, on the plan. 3. A copy of the petition of the trustees. 4. A copy of the act we wished from the Legislature. They are long; but as we always counted on you as the main pillar of their support, and we shall probably return to the charge at the next session, the trouble of reading them will come upon you, and as well now as then. The lottery allowed by the former act, the proceeds of our two glebes, and our dividend of the Literary Fund, with the re-organization of the institution, are what was asked in that petition. In addition to this, if we could obtain a loan for four or five years only of seven or eight thousand dollars, I think I have it now in my power to obtain three of the ablest characters in the world to fill the higher professorships of what in the plan is called the second, or general grade of education; three such characters as are not in a single University of Europe; and for those of languages and mathematics, a part of the same grade, able professors doubtless could also be readily obtained. With these characters, I should not be afraid to say that the circle of the sciences composing that second, or general grade, would be more profoundly taught here than in any institution in the United States, and I might go farther. The first, or elementary grade of education is not developed in this plan; an authority only being asked to its Visitors for putting into motion a former proposition for that object. For an explanation of this, therefore, I am obliged to add to these papers a letter I wrote some time since to Mr. Adams,† in which I had occasion to give some account of what had been proposed here for culling from every condition of our people the natural aristocracy of talents and virtue, and of preparing it by education, at the public expense, for the care of the public concerns.

* The documents referred to in this letter do not appear to be available. One can assume that the ideas contained in them were similar to those outlined to Cooper and Carr, Appendixes X and XI [J. B. C.].
† See Appendix IX.

APPENDIX XIII

EXTRACT FROM A LETTER TO JOSEPH C. CABELL
FROM MONTICELLO, FEBRUARY 2, 1816
(Honeywell, Appendix F, pp. 228–229; Cabell, pp. 53–58)

My letter of the 24th ult. conveyed to you the grounds of the two articles objected to in the College bill. Your last presents one of them in a new point of view, that of the commencement of the Ward schools as likely to render the law unpopular to the county. It must be a very inconsiderate and rough process of execution that would do this. My idea of the mode of carrying it into execution would be this. Declare the counties *ipso facto* divided into wards, for the present by the boundaries of the militia captaincies; somebody attend the ordinary muster of each company, having first desired the Captain to call together a full one. There explain the object of the law to the people of the company, put to their vote whether they will have a school established, and the most central and convenient place for it; get them to meet and build a log school house, have a roll taken of the children who would attend it, and of those of them able to pay. These would probably be sufficient to support a common teacher, instructing gratis the few unable to pay. If there should be a deficiency, it would require too trifling a contribution from the county to be complained of; and especially as the whole county would participate, where necessary, in the same resource. Should the company, by it's vote, decide that it would have no school, let them remain without one. The advantages of this proceeding would be, that it would become the duty of the aldermen elected by the county to take an active part in pressing the introduction of schools and to look out for tutors. If however it is intended that the State government shall take this business into it's own hands, and provide schools for every county, then by all means strike out this provision of our bill. I would never wish that it should be placed on a worse footing than the rest of the state. But if it is believed that these elementary schools will be better managed by the Governor and council, the Commissioners of the literary fund, or any other general authority of the government, than by the parents within each ward, it is a belief against all experience. Try the principle one step further, and amend the bill so as to commit to the Governor and Council the management of all our farms, our mills, and merchants' stores. No, my friend, the way to have good and safe government, is not to trust it all to one; but to divide it among the many, distributing to every one exactly the functions he is competent to. Let the National government be entrusted with the defence of the nation and it's foreign and federal relations; the State governments with the civil rights, laws, police and administration of what concerns the State generally; the Counties with the local concerns of the counties; and each Ward direct the interests within itself. It is by dividing and subdividing these republics from the great National one down thro' all its subordinations, until it ends in the administration of every man's farm and affairs by himself; by placing under every one what his own eye may superintend, that all will be done for the best. What has destroyed liberty and the rights of man in every government which has ever existed under the sun? The generalizing and concentrating all cares and powers into one body, no matter whether of the autocrats of Russia or France, or the aristocrats of a Venetian Senate. And I do belief that if the Almighty has not decreed that Man shall never be free, (and it is blasphemy to believe it,) that the secret will be found to be in the making himself the depository of the powers respecting himself, so far as he is competent to them, and delegating only what is beyond his competence by a synthetical process, to higher and higher orders of functionaries, so as to trust fewer and fewer powers, in proportion as the trustees become more and more oligarchical. The elementary republics of the wards, the county republics, the State republics and the republic of the Union, would form a gradation of authorities, standing each on the basis of law, holding every one it's delegated share of powers, and constituting truly a system of fundamental balances and checks for the government. Where every man is a sharer in the direction of his ward republic, or of some of the higher ones, and feels that he is a participator in the government of affairs not merely at an election, one day in the year, but every day; when there shall not be a man in the state who will not be a member of some one of it's councils, great or small, he will let the heart be torn out of his body, sooner than his power be wrested from him by a Caesar or a Bonaparte. How powerfully did we feel the energy of this organization in the case of the Embargo? I felt the foundations of the Government shaken under my feet by the New England townships. There was not an individual in their states whose body was not thrown, with all it's momentum, into action, and, altho' the whole of the other states were known to be in favor of the measure, yet the organization of this little selfish minority enabled it to overrule the Union. What could the unwieldy counties of the middle, the South and the West do? Call a county meeting, and the drunken loungers at and about the Courthouses would have collected, the distances being too great for the good people and the industrious generally to attend. The character of those who really met would have been the measure of the weight they would have had in the scale of public opinion. As Cato then concluded every speech with the words 'Carthago delenda est,' so do I every opinion with the injunction 'divide the counties into wards.' Begin them only for a single purpose; they will soon shew for what others they are best instruments. God bless you, and all our rulers, and give them the wisdom, as I am sure they have the will, to fortify us against the degeneracy of our government, and the concentration of all it's powers in the hands of the one, the few, the well-born, or but the many.

APPENDIX XIV

EXTRACT FROM A LETTER TO GOVERNOR WILSON C. NICHOLAS, APRIL 2, 1816 *

(Honeywell, Appendix G, pp. 230–232; Cabell, Introduction, p. xxxii)

The President and Directors of the literary fund are desired to digest and report a system of public education, comprehending the establishment of an university, additional colleges or academies, and schools. The resolution does not define the portions of science to be taught in each of these institutions, but the first and last admit no doubt. The university must be intended for all useful sciences, and the schools mean elementary ones, for the instruction of the people, answering to our present English schools; the middle term, colleges or academies, may be more conjectural. But we must understand

* Governor Nicholas, as president of the directors of the Literary Fund and pursuant to a resolution of the Virginia legislature, was inquiring into plans for the best expenditure of the income of this fund for educational purposes [J. B. C.].

from it some middle grade of education. Now, when we advert that the ancient classical languages are considered as the foundation preparatory for all the sciences; that we have always had schools scattered over the country for teaching these languages, which often were the ultimate term of education; that these languages are entered on at the age of nine or ten years, at which age parents would be unwilling to send their children from every part of the State to a central and distant university, and when we observe that the resolution supposes there are to be a plurality of them, we may well conclude that the Greek and Latin are the objects of these colleges. It is probable, also, that the legislature might have under their eye the bill for the more general diffusion of knowledge,† printed in the revised code of 1779, which proposed these three grades of institution, to wit: an university, district colleges, or grammar schools, and county or ward schools. I think, therefore, we may say that the object of these colleges is the classical languages, and that they are intended as the portico of entry to the university. As to their numbers, I know no better rule to be assumed than to place one within a day's ride of every man's door, in consideration of the infancy of the pledges he has at it. This would require one for every eighty miles square.

Supposing this the object of the colleges, the report will have to present the plan of an university, analyzing the sciences, selecting those which are useful, grouping them into professorships, commensurate each with the time and faculties of one man, and prescribing the regimen and all other necessary details. On this subject 1 can offer nothing new. A letter of mine to Peter Carr,‡ which was published during the last session of Assembly, is a digest of all the information I possess on the subject, from which the Board will judge whether they can extract anything useful; the professorship of the classical languages being of course to be expunged, as more effectually supplied by the establishment of the colleges.

As the buildings to be erected will also enter into their report, I would strongly recommend to their consideration, instead of one immense building, to have a small one for every professorship, arranged at proper distances around a square, or rather three sides of a square, to admit extension, connected by a piazza, so that they may go dry from one school to another. This village form is preferable to a single great building for many reasons, particularly on account of fire, health, economy, peace and quiet. Such a plan had been approved in the case of the Albemarle College, which was the subject of the letter above mentioned; and should the idea be approved by the Board, more may be said hereafter on the opportunity these small buildings will afford, of exhibiting models in architecture of the purest forms of antiquity, furnishing to the student examples of the precepts he will be taught in that art.

The Elementary or Ward schools are the last branch of this subject; on this, too, my ideas have been long deposited in the bill for the diffusion of knowledge, before mentioned, and time and reflection have continued to strengthen them as to the general principle, that of a division of every county into wards, with a school in each ward. The details of the bill will of course

† See Appendix I.
‡ See Appendix XI.

be varied as the difference of present circumstances from those of that day will require.

My partiality for that division is not founded in views of education solely, but infinitely more as the means of a better administration of our government, and the eternal preservation of its republican principles. The example of this most admirable of all human contrivances in government, is to be seen in our Eastern States; and its powerful effect in the order and economy of their internal affairs, and the momentum it gives them as a nation, is the single circumstance which distinguishes them so remarkably from every other national association. In a letter to Mr. Adams a few years ago,§ I had occasion to explain to him the structure of our scheme of education as proposed in the bill for the diffusion of knowledge, and the views of this particular section of it; and in another lately to Mr. Cabell,|| on the occasion of the bill for the Albemarle College, I also took a view of the political effects of the proposed division into wards, which being more easily copied than thrown into new form here, I take the liberty of enclosing extracts from them. Should the Board of Directors approve of the plan, and make ward divisions the substratum of their elementary schools, their report may furnish a happy occasion of introducing them, leaving all their other uses to be adapted from time to time hereafter as occasions shall occur.

§ See Appendix IX.
|| See Appendix XIII.

APPENDIX XV

PORTIONS OF JEFFERSON'S BILLS FOR ESTABLISHING SCHOOLS,
COLLEGES, AND A UNIVERSITY, OCTOBER 24, 1817

(Honeywell, Appendix H, pp. 233–243; Padover, pp. 1072–1076)

On September 9, 1817, Jefferson sent to Cabell the draft of a bill for the establishment of elementary schools. Soon afterward he prepared bills for district colleges and a university. These he combined into a Bill for Establishing a System of Public Education, which he sent to Cabell on October 24.

[Sections 1 and 2 provide that the judge in every county is to appoint three Visitors to the elementary schools in his county, and regulate the way in which the Visitors shall divide the county into wards "so designated as to comprehend each, about the number of militia sufficient for a company."]

3. The original division into wards being made, the Visitors shall appoint days for the first meeting of every ward, at such place as they shall name within the same, of which appointment notice shall be given at least two weeks before the day of meeting, by advertisement at some public place within the ward, requiring every free, white male citizen, of full age, resident

within the ward, to meet at the place, and by the hour of twelve of the day so appointed, at which meeting some one of the Visitors shall also attend, and a majority of the said warders being in attendance, the Visitor present shall propose to them to decide by a majority of their votes,—1. The location of a school-house for the ward, and a dwelling-house for the teacher (the owner of the ground consenting thereto). 2. The size and structure of the said houses; and 3. Whether the same shall be built by the joint labor of the warders, or by their pecuniary contributions; and also 4. To elect by a plurality of their votes a warden, resident, who shall direct and superintend the said buildings, and be charged with their future care.

4. And if they decide that the said buildings shall be erected by the joint labor of the warders, then all persons within the said ward liable to work in the highways, shall attend at the order of the warden, and, under his direction, shall labor thereon until completed, under the same penalties as provided by law to enforce labor on the highways. And if they decide on erection by pecuniary contributions, the residents and owners of property within the ward shall contribute toward the cost, each in proportion to the taxes they last paid to the State for their persons and for the same property: . . .

5. It shall be the duty of the said Visitors to seek and to employ for every ward,* whenever the number and ages of its children require it, a person of

* Estimating eight hundred militia to a county, there will be twelve captaincies or wards in a county on an average. Suppose each of these, three years in every six, to have children enough for a school, who have not yet had three years' schooling; such a county will employ six teachers, each serving two wards by alternate terms. These teachers will be taken from the laboring classes, as they are now, to wit: from that which furnishes mechanics, overseers and tillers of the earth; and they will chiefly be the cripples, the weakly and the old, of that class, who will have been qualified for these functions by the ward schools themselves. If put on a footing then, for wages and subsistence, with the young and the able of their class, they will be liberally compensated: say with one hundred and fifty dollars wages and the usual allowance of meat and bread. The subsistence will probably be contributed in kind by the warders, out of their family stock. The wages alone will be a pecuniary tax of about nine hundred dollars. To a county, this addition would be of about one-fifth of the taxes we now pay to the State, or about one-fifth of one per cent on every man's taxable property; if tax can be called that which we give to our children in the most valuable of all forms, that of instruction. Were those schools to be established on the public funds, and to be managed by the Governor and council, or the commissioners of the Literary fund, brick houses to be built for the schools and teachers, high wages and subsistence given them, they would be badly managed, depraved by abuses, and would exhaust the whole Literary fund. While under the eye and animadversion of the wards, and the control of the wardens and visitors, economy, diligence, and correctness of conduct, will be enforced, the whole Literary fund will be spared to complete the general system of education, by colleges in every district for instruction in the languages, and an university for the whole of the higher sciences; and this, by an addition to our contributions almost insensible, and which, in fact, will not be felt as a burthen, because applied immediately and visibly to the good of our children.

A question of some doubt might be raised on the latter part of this section, as to the rights and duties of society towards its members, infant and adult. Is it a right or a duty in society to take care of their infant members in opposition to good moral character, qualified to teach reading, writing, numeral arithmetic and geography, whose subsistence shall be furnished by the residents and proprietors of the ward, either in money or in kind, at the choice of each contributor, and in the ratio of their public taxes, to be apportioned and levied as on the failures before provided for. The teacher shall also have the use of the house and accommodations provided for him, and shall moreover receive annually such standing wages as the Visitors shall have determined to be proportioned on the residents and proprietors of the ward, and to be paid, levied and applied as before provided in other cases of pecuniary contribution.

6. At this school shall be received and instructed gratis, every infant of competent age who has not already had three years' schooling. And it is declared and enacted, that no person unborn or under the age of twelve years at the passing of this act, and who is *compos mentis,* shall, after the age of fifteen years, be a citizen of this commonwealth until he or she can read readily in some tongue, native or acquired.

[Sections 7-9 concern the administrative duties of the Visitors and the regulation of the ward meetings.]

10. When, on the application of any warden, authorized thereto by the vote of his ward, the judge of the Superior Court shall be of opinion that the contributors of any particular ward are disproportionably and oppressively overburthened with an unusual number of children of non-contributors of their ward, he may direct an order to the county court to assess in their next county levy the whole or such part of the extra burthen as he shall think excessive and unreasonable, to be paid to the warden for its proper use, to which order the said county court is required to conform.

11. The said teachers shall, in all things relating to the education and government of their pupils, be under the direction and control of the Visitors; but no religious reading, instruction or exercise, shall be prescribed or practiced inconsistent with the tenets of any religious sect or denomination.

12. Some one of the Visitors, once in every year at least, shall visit the several schools: shall inquire into the proceedings and practices thereat: shall examine the progress of the pupils, and give to those who excel in reading, in writing, in arithmetic, or in geography, such honorary marks and testimonies of approbation, as may encourage and excite to industry and emulation.

----

the will of the parent? How far does this right and duty extend?—to guard the life of the infant, his property, his instruction, his morals? The Roman father was supreme in all these: we draw a line, but where?—public sentiment does not seem to have traced it precisely. Nor is it necessary in the present case. It is better to tolerate the rare instance of a parent refusing to let his child be educated, than to shock the common feelings and ideas by the forcible asportation and education of the infant against the will of the father. What is proposed here is to remove the objection of expense, by offering education gratis, and to strengthen parental excitement by the disfranchisement of his child while uneducated. Society has certainly a right to disavow him whom they offer, and are not permitted to qualify for the duties of a citizen. If we do not force instruction, let us at least strengthen the motives to receive it when offered [T. J.].

13. All decisions and proceedings of the Visitors relative to the original designation of wards at any time before the buildings are begun, or changes of wards at any time after, to the quantum of subsistence, or wages allowed to the teacher, and to the rules prescribed to him for the education and government of his pupils, shall be subject to be controlled and corrected by the judge of the Superior Court of the county, on the complaint of any individual aggrieved or interested.

[Section 14 directs the distribution of nine collegiate districts among the counties, and Section 15 provides for the appointment of a Board of Visitors for each college district, by the President and Directors of the Literary Fund.]

16. The said Visitors, or so many of them as, being a majority, shall attend, shall appoint a rector, of their own body, who shall preside at their meetings, and a secretary to record and preserve their proceedings; and shall proceed to consider of the site for a college most convenient for their district, having regard to the extent, population and other circumstances, . . .

[Section 17 deals with the procurement of land for the college.]

18. On each of the sites so located shall be erected one or more substantial buildings—the walls of which shall be of brick or stone, with two school rooms, and four rooms for the accommodation of the professors, and with sixteen dormitories in or adjacent to the same, each sufficient for two pupils, and in which no more than two shall be permitted to lodge, with a fireplace in each, and the whole in a comfortable and decent style, suitable to their purpose.

[Sections 19 and 20 are concerned with the building and naming of the colleges.]

21. In the said colleges shall be taught the Greek, Latin, French, Spanish, Italian and German languages, English grammar, geography, ancient and modern, the higher branches of numerical arithmetic, the mensuration of land, the use of the globes, and the ordinary elements of navigation.

22. To each of the said colleges shall be appointed two professors, the one for teaching Greek, Latin, and such other branches of learning before described thereof . . .

[Two alternative schemes for establishing a university "in a central and healthy part of the state" are provided; both involve the conversion of Central College in Albemarle County into the university. The Board of Visitors for the university is to be appointed by the officers of the Literary Fund, who are to become a Board of Public Instruction.]

34. In the said University shall be taught history and geography, ancient and modern; natural philosophy, agriculture, chemistry and the theories of medicine; anatomy, zoology, botany, mineralogy and geology; mathematics, pure and mixed; military and naval science; ideology, ethics, the law of nature and of nations; law, municipal and foreign; the science of civil government and political economy; languages, rhetoric, belles lettres, and the

fine arts generally; which branches of science shall be so distributed and under so many professorships, not exceeding ten, as the Visitors shall think most proper.

35. Each professor shall be allowed the use of the apartments and accommodations provided for him, and such standing salary, not exceeding $1,000 yearly, as the Visitors shall think proper, to be drawn from the literary fund, with such tuition fees from the students as the Visitors shall establish.

[Then follow a number of sections dealing with the duties of the Board of Visitors of the university. In the last section (42, which follows), Jefferson proves his continuing loyalty to his selective scholarship scheme of 1779.]

And to avail the Commonwealth of those talents and virtues which nature has sown as liberally among the poor as rich, and which are lost to their country by the want of means for their cultivation, Be it further enacted as follows:

42. On every 29th day of February, or, if that be Sunday, then on the next day, the Visitors of the Ward-schools in every county shall meet at the Court-House of their county, and after the most diligent and impartial observation and enquiry of the boys who have been three years at the Ward-schools, and whose parents are too poor to give them a collegiate education, shall select from among them some one of the most promising and sound understanding, who shall be sent to the first meeting of the Visitors of their collegiate district, with such proofs as the case requires and admits, for the examination and information of that Board; who, from among the candidates so offered from the several counties of their district, shall select two of the most sound and promising understanding, who shall be admitted to their College, and there be maintained and educated five years at the public expense, under such rules and limitations as the Board of Public Instruction shall prescribe; and at the end of the said five years the said Collegiate Visitors shall select that one of the two who shall, on their most diligent and impartial enquiry and best information, be adjudged by them to be of the most sound and promising understanding and character, and most improved by their course of education, who shall be sent on immediately thereafter to the University, there to be maintained and educated in such branches of the sciences taught there as are most proper to qualify him for the calling to which his parents or guardians may destine him; and to continue at the said University three years at the public expense, under such rules and limitations as the Board of Public Instruction shall prescribe. And the expenses of the persons so to be publicly maintained and educated at the Colleges and University shall be drawn by their respective Visitors from the literary fund.

Appendixes

APPENDIX XVI

EXTRACT FROM A LETTER TO J. CORREA DE SERRA
FROM POPLAR FOREST, VIRGINIA, NOVEMBER 25, 1817
(Lipscomb, vol. XV, pp. 153–157)

I find from his [Dr. Thomas Cooper's] information that we are not to expect to obtain in this country either a classical or mathematical professor of the first order; and as our institution cannot be raised above the common herd of academies, colleges, etc., already scattered over our country, but by supereminent professors, we have determined to accept of no mediocrity, and to seek in Europe-for what is eminent. We shall go to Edinburgh in preference, because of the advantage to students of receiving communications in their native tongue, and because peculiar and personal circumstances will enable us to interest Dugald Stewart and Professor Leslie, of that College, in procuring us subjects of real worth and eminence. I put off writing to them for a classical and mathematical professor only until I see what our legislature, which meets on Monday next, is disposed to do, either on the question singly of adopting our college for their university, or on that of entering at once on a general system of instruction, for which they have for some time been preparing. For this last purpose I have sketched, and put into the hands of a member a bill, delineating a practicable plan, entirely within the means they already have on hand, destined to this object. My bill proposes, 1. Elementary schools in every county, which shall place every householder within three miles of a school. 2. District colleges, which shall place every father within a day's ride of a college where he may dispose of his son. 3. An university in a healthy and central situation, with the offer of the lands, buildings, and funds of the Central College, if they will accept that place for their establishment. In the first will be taught reading, writing, common arithmetic, and general notions of geography. In the second, ancient and modern languages, geography fully, a higher degree of numerical arithmetic, mensuration, and the elementary principles of navigation. In the third, all the useful sciences in their highest degree. To all of which is added a selection from the elementary schools of subjects of the most promising genius, whose parents are too poor to give them further education, to be carried at the public expense through the colleges and university. The object is to bring into action that mass of talents which lies buried in poverty in every country, for want of the means of development, and thus give activity to a mass of mind, which, in proportion to our population, shall be the double or treble of what it is in most countries. The expense of the elementary schools for every county, is proposed to be levied on the wealth of the county, and all children rich and poor to be educated at these three years gratis. The expense of the colleges and university, admitting two professors to each of the former, and ten to the latter, can be completely and permanently established with a sum of five hundred thousand dollars, in addition to the present funds of our Central College. Our literary fund has already on hand, and appropriated to these purposes, a sum of seven hundred thousand dollars, and that increasing yearly. This is in fact and substance the plan I proposed in a bill forty years ago, but accommodated to the circumstances of this, instead of that day. I derive my present hopes that it may now be adopted, from the fact that the House of Representatives, at their last session, passed a bill, less practicable and boundlessly expensive, and therefore alone rejected by the Senate, and printed for public consideration and amendment.* Mine, after all, may be an Utopian dream, but being innocent, I have thought I might indulge in it till I go to the land of dreams, and sleep there with the dreamers of all past and future times.

* The bill referred to is Mercer's bill (Appendix XXVI). It is interesting that in this letter Jefferson states only that the bill was "less practicable and boundlessly expensive" [J. B. C.].

APPENDIX XVII

REPORT OF THE COMMISSIONERS APPOINTED TO FIX THE SITE OF THE UNIVERSITY OF VIRGINIA, AUGUST 1, 1818

(Honeywell, Appendix J, pp. 248–260; Padover, pp. 1097–1105)

The Commissioners for the University of Virginia, having met, as by law required, at the tavern, in Rockfish Gap, on the Blue Ridge, on the first day of August, of this present year, 1818; and having formed a board, proceeded on that day to the discharge of the duties assigned to them by the act of the Legislature, entitled "An act, appropriating part of the revenue of the literary fund, and for other purposes"; and having continued their proceedings by adjournment, from day to day, to Tuesday, the 4th day of August, have agreed to a report on the several matters with which they were charged, which report they now respectfully address and submit to the Legislature of the State.

The first duty enjoined on them, was to enquire and report a site, in some convenient and proper part of the State, for an university, to be called the "University of Virginia." In this enquiry, they supposed that the governing considerations should be the healthiness of the site, the fertility of the neighboring county, and its centrality to the white population of the whole State. For, although the act authorized and required them to receive any voluntary contributions, whether conditional or absolute, which might be offered through them to the President and Directors of the Literary Fund, for the benefit of the University, yet they did not consider this as establishing an auction, or as pledging the location to the highest bidder.

Three places were proposed, to wit: Lexington, in the county of Rockbridge, Staunton, in the county of Augusta, and the Central College, in the county of Albemarle. Each of these was unexceptionable as to healthiness and fertility. It was the degree of centrality to the white population of the State which alone then constituted the important point of comparison between these places; and the Board, after full enquiry, and impartial and mature consideration, are of opinion, that the central point of the white population of the State is nearer to the Central College than to either Lexington or Staunton, by great and important differences; and all other circumstances of the place in general being favorable to it, as a position for an university, they do report the Central College in Albemarle, to be a convenient and proper part of the State for the University of Virginia.

2. The Board having thus agreed on a proper site for the University, to be reported to the Legislature, proceed to the second of the duties assigned to them—that of proposing a plan for its buildings—and they are of opinion that it should consist of distinct houses or pavilions, arranged at proper distances on each side of a lawn of a proper breadth, and of indefinite extent, in one direction, at least; in each of which should be a lecturing room, with from two to four apartments, for the accommodation of a professor and his family; that these pavilions should be united by a range of dormitories, sufficient each for the accommodation of two students only, this provision being deemed advantageous to morals, to order, and to uninterrupted study; and that a passage of some kind, under cover from the weather, should give a communication along the whole range. It is supposed that such pavilions, on an average of the larger and smaller, will cost each about $5,000; each dormitory about $350, and hotels of a single room, for a refectory, and two rooms for the tenant, necessary for dieting the students, will cost about $3,500 each. The number of these pavilions will depend on the number of professors, and that of the dormitories and hotels on the number of students to be lodged and dieted. The advantages of this plan are: greater security against fire and infection; tranquillity and comfort to the professors and their families thus insulated; retirement to the students; and the admission of enlargment to any degree to which the institution may extend in future times. It is supposed probable, that a building of somewhat more size in the middle of the grounds may be called for in time, in which may be rooms for religious worship, under such impartial regulations as the Visitors shall prescribe, for public examinations, for a library, for the schools of music, drawing, and other associated purposes.

3, 4. In proceeding to the third and fourth duties prescribed by the Legislature, of reporting "the branches of learning, which should be taught in the University, and the number and description of the professorships they will require," the Commissioners were first to consider at what point it was understood that university education should commence? Certainly not with the alphabet, for reasons of expediency and impracticability, as well from the obvious sense of the Legislature, who, in the same act, make other provision for the primary instruction of the poor children, expecting, doubtless, that in other cases it would be provided by the parent, or become, perhaps, subject of future and further attention of the Legislature. The objects of this primary education determine its character and limits. These objects would be,

To give to every citizen the information he needs for the transaction of his own business;

To enable him to calculate for himself, and to express and preserve his ideas, his contracts and accounts, in writing;

To improve, by reading, his morals and faculties;

To understand his duties to his neighbors and country, and to discharge with competence the functions confided to him by either;

To know his rights; to exercise with order and justice those he retains; to choose with discretion the fiduciary of those he delegates; and to notice their conduct with diligence, with candor, and judgment;

And, in general, to observe with intelligence and faithfulness all the social relations under which he shall be placed.

To instruct the mass of our citizens in these, their rights, interests and duties, as men and citizens, being then the objects of education in the primary schools, whether private or public, in them should be taught reading, writing and numerical arithmetic, the elements of mensuration (useful in so many callings,) and the outlines of geography and history. And this brings us to the point at which are to commence the higher branches of education, of which the Legislature require the development; those, for example, which are,

To form the statesmen, legislators and judges, on whom public prosperity and individual happiness are so much to depend;

To expound the principles and structure of government, the laws which regulate the intercourse of nations, those formed municipally for our own government, and a sound spirit of legislation, which, banishing all arbitrary and unnecessary restraint on individual action, shall leave us free to do whatever does not violate the equal rights of another;

To harmonize and promote the interests of agriculture, manufactures and commerce, and by well informed views of political economy to give a free scope to the public industry;

To develop the reasoning faculties of our youth, enlarge their minds, cultivate their morals, and instill into them the precepts of virtue and order;

To enlighten them with mathematical and physical sciences, which advance the arts, and administer to the health, the subsistence, and comforts of human life;

And, generally, to form them to habits of reflection and correct action, rendering them examples of virtue to others, and of happiness within themselves.

These are the objects of that higher grade of education, the benefits and blessings of which the Legislature now propose to provide for the good and ornament of their country, the gratification and happiness of their fellow-citizens, of the parent especially, and his progeny, on which all his affections are concentrated.

In entering on this field, the Commissioners are aware that they have to encounter much difference of opinion as to the extent which it is expedient that this institution should occupy. Some good men, and even of respectable information, consider the learned sciences as useless acquirements; some think that they do not better the conditions of man; and others that education, like private and individual concerns, should be left to private individual efforts; not reflecting that an establishment embracing all the sciences which may be useful and even necessary in the various vocations of life, with the buildings and apparatus belonging to each, are far beyond the reach of individual means, and must either derive existence from public patronage, or not exist at all. This would leave us, then, without those callings which depend on education, or send us to other countries to seek the instruction they require. But the Commissioners are happy in considering the statute under which they are assembled as proof that the Legislature is far from the abandonment of objects so interesting. They are sensible that the advantages of well-directed education, moral, political and economical, are truly above all estimate. Education generates habits of application, of order, and the love of virtue; and controls, by the force of habit, any innate obliquities in our moral organization. We should be far, too, from the discouraging persuasion that man is fixed, by the law of his nature, at a given point; that his improvement is a chimera, and the hope delusive of rendering ourselves wiser, happier or better than our forefathers were. As well might it be urged that the wild and uncultivated tree, hitherto yielding sour and bitter fruit only, can never be made to yield better; yet we know that the grafting art implants a new tree on the savage stock, producing what is most estimable both in kind and degree. Education, in like manner, engrafts a new man on the native stock, and improves what in his nature was vicious and perverse into qualities of virtue and social worth. And it cannot be but that each generation succeeding to the knowledge acquired by all those who preceded it, adding to it their own acquisitions and discoveries, and handing the mass down for successive and constant accumulation, must advance the knowledge and well-being of mankind, not *infinitely*, as some have said, but *indefinitely*, and to a term which no one can fix and foresee. Indeed, we need look back half a century, to times which many now living remember well, and see the wonderful advances in the sciences and arts which have been made within that period. Some of these have rendered the elements themselves subservient to the purposes of man, have harnessed them to the yoke of his labors, and effected the great blessings of moderating his own, of accomplishing what was beyond his feeble force, and extending the comforts of life to a much enlarged circle, to those who had before known its necessaries only. That these are not the vain dreams of sanguine hope, we have before our eyes real and living examples. What, but education, has advanced us beyond the condition of our indigenous neighbors? And what chains them to their present state of barbarism and wretchedness, but a bigotted veneration for the supposed superlative wisdom of their fathers, and the preposterous idea that they are to look backward for better things, and not forward, longing, as it should seem, to return to the days of eating acorns and roots, rather than indulge in the degeneracies of civilization? And how much more encouraging to the achievements of science and improvement is this, than the desponding view that the condition of man cannot be ameliorated, that what has been must ever be, and that to secure ourselves where we are, we must tread with awful reverence in the footsteps of our fathers. This doctrine is the genuine fruit of the alliance between Church and State; the tenants of which, finding themselves but too well in their present condition, oppose all advances which might unmask their usurpations, and monopolies of honors, wealth, and power, and fear every change, as endangering the comforts they now hold. Nor must we omit to mention, among the benefits of education, the incalculable advantage of training up able counsellors to administer the affairs of our country in all its departments, legislative, executive and judiciary, and to bear their proper share in the councils of our national government; nothing more than education advancing the prosperity, the power, and the happiness of a nation.

Encouraged, therefore, by the sentiments of the Legislature, manifested in this statute, we present the following tabular statements of the branches of learning which we think should be taught in the University, forming them into groups, each of which are within the powers of a single professor:

I. Languages, ancient:
   Latin,
   Greek,
   Hebrew.
II. Languages, modern:
   French,
   Spanish,
   Italian,
   German,
   Anglo-Saxon.
III. Mathematics, pure:
   Algebra,
   Fluxions,
   Geometry, Elementary,
      Transcendental.
   Architecture, Military,
      Naval.
IV. Physico-Mathematics:
   Mechanics,
   Statics,
   Dynamics,
   Pneumatics,
   Acoustics,
   Optics,
   Astronomy,
   Geography.
V. Physics, or Natural Philosophy:
   Chemistry,
   Mineralogy.
VI. Botany,
   Zoölogy.
VII. Anatomy,
   Medicine.
VIII. Government,
   Political Economy,
   Law of Nature and Nations,
   History, being interwoven
      with Politics and Law.
IX. Law, municipal.
X. Idealogy,
   General Grammar,
   Ethics,
   Rhetoric,
   Belles Letters, and the fine arts.

Some of the terms used in this table being subject to a difference of acceptation, it is proper to define the meaning and comprehension intended to be given them here:

Geometry, Elementary, is that of straight lines and of the circle.

Transcendental, is that of all other curves; it includes, of course, *Projectiles*, a leading branch of the military art.

Military Architecture includes Fortification, another branch of that art.

Statics respect matter generally, in a state of rest, and include Hydrostatics, or the laws of fluids particularly, at rest or in equilibrio.

Dynamics, used as a general term, include Dynamics proper, or the laws of *solids* in motion; and Hydrodynamics, or Hydraulics, those of *fluids* in motion.

Pneumatics teach the theory of air, its weight, motion, condensation, rarefaction, etc.

Acoustics, or Phonics, the theory of sound.

Optics, the laws of light and vision.

Physics, or Physiology, in a general sense, mean the doctrine of the physical objects of our senses.

Chemistry is meant, with its other usual branches, to comprehend the theory of agriculture.

Mineralogy, in addition to its peculiar subjects, is here understood to embrace what is real in geology.

Ideology is the doctrine of thought.

General Grammar explains the construction of language.

Some articles in this distribution of sciences will need observation. A professor is proposed for ancient languages, the Latin, Greek, and Hebrew, particularly; but these languages being the foundation common to all the sciences, it is difficult to foresee what may be the extent of this school. At the same time, no greater obstruction to industrious study could be proposed than the presence, the intrusions and the noisy turbulence of a multitude of small boys; and if they are to be placed here for the rudiments of the languages, they may be so numerous that its character and value as an University will be merged in those of a Grammar school. It is, therefore, greatly to be wished, that preliminary schools, either on private or public establishment, could be distributed in districts through the State, as preparatory to the entrance of students into the University. The tender age at which this part of education commences, generally about the tenth year, would weigh heavily with parents in sending their sons to a school so distant as the central establishment would be from most of them. Districts of such extent as that every parent should be within a day's journey of his son at school, would be desirable in cases of sickness, and convenient for supplying their ordinary wants, and might be made to lessen sensibly the expense of this part of their education. And where a spare population would not, within such a compass, furnish subjects sufficient to maintain a school, a competent enlargement of district must, of necessity, there be submitted to. At these district schools or colleges, boys should be rendered able to read the easier authors, Latin and Greek. This would be useful and sufficient for many not intended for an University education. At these, too, might be taught English grammar, the higher branches of numerical arithmetic, the geometry of straight lines and of the circle, the elements of navigation, and geography to a sufficient degree, and thus afford to greater numbers the means of being qualified for the various vocations of life, needing more instruction than merely menial or praedial labor, and the same advantages to youths whose education may have been neglected until too late to lay a foundation in the learned languages. These institutions, intermediate between the primary schools and University, might then be the passage of entrance for youths into the University, where their classical learning might be critically completed, by a study of the authors of highest degree; and it is at this stage only that they should be received at the University. Giving then a portion of their time to a finishing knowledge of the Latin and Greek, the rest might be appropriated to the modern languages, or to the commencement of the course of science for which they should be destined.

This would generally be about the fifteenth year of their age, when they might go with more safety and contentment to that distance from their parents. Until this preparatory provision shall be made, either the University will be overwhelmed with the grammar school, or a separate establishment, under one or more ushers, for its lower classes, will be advisable, at a mile or two distance from the general one; where, too, may be exercised the stricter government necessary for young boys, but unsuitable for youths arrived at years of discretion.

The considerations which have governed the specification of languages to be taught by the professor of modern languages were, that the French is the language of general intercourse among nations, and as a depository of human science, is unsurpassed by any other language, living or dead; that the Spanish is highly interesting to us, as the language spoken by so great a portion of the inhabitants of our continents, with whom we shall probably have great intercourse ere long, and is that also in which is written the greater part of the earlier history of America. The Italian abounds with works of very superior order, valuable for their matter, and still more distinguished as models of the finest taste in style and composition. And the German now stands in a line with that of the most learned nations in richness of erudition and advance in the sciences. It is too of common descent with the language of our own country, a branch of the same original Gothic stock, and furnishes valuable illustrations for us. But in this point of view, the Anglo-Saxon is of peculiar value. We have placed it among the modern languages, because it is in fact that which we speak, in the earliest form in which we have knowledge of it. It has been undergoing, with time, those gradual changes which all languages, ancient and modern, have experienced; and even now needs only to be printed in the modern character and orthography to be intelligible, in a considerable degree, to an English reader. It has this value, too, above the Greek and Latin, that while it gives the radix of the mass of our language, they explain its innovations only. Obvious proofs of this have been presented to the modern reader in the disquisitions of Horn Tooke; and Fortescue Aland has well explained the great instruction which may be derived from it to a full understanding of our ancient common law, on which, as a stock, our whole system of law is engrafted. It will form the first link in the chain of an historical review of our language through all its successive changes to the present day, will constitute the foundation of that critical instruction in it which ought to be found in a seminary of general learning, and thus reward amply the few weeks of attention which would alone be requisite for its attainment; a language already fraught with all the eminent science of our parent country, the future vehicle of whatever we may ourselves achieve, and destined to occupy so much space on the globe, claims distinguished attention in American education.

Medicine, where fully taught, is usually subdivided into several professorships, but this cannot well be without the accessory of an hospital, where the student can have the benefit of attending clinical lectures, and of assisting at operations of surgery. With this accessory, the seat of our University is not yet prepared, either by its population or by the numbers of poor who would leave their own houses, and accept of the charities of an hospital. For the present, therefore, we propose but a single professor for both medicine and anatomy. By him the medical science may be taught, with a history and explanations of all its successive theories from Hippocrates to the present day; and anatomy may be fully treated. Vegetable pharmacy will make a part of the botanical course, and mineral and chemical pharmacy of those of mineralogy and chemistry. This degree of medical information is such as the mass of scientific students would wish to possess, as enabling them in their course through life, to estimate with satisfaction the extent and limits of the aid to human life and health, which they may understandingly expect from that art; and it constitutes such a foundation for those intended for the profession, that the finishing course of practice at the bed-sides of the sick, and at the operations of surgery in a hospital, can neither be long nor expensive. To seek this finishing elsewhere, must therefore be submitted to for a while.

In conformity with the principles of our Constitution, which places all sects of religion on an equal footing, with the jealousies of the different sects in guarding that equality from encroachment and surprise, and with the sentiments of the Legislature in favor of freedom of religion, manifested on former occasions, we have proposed no professor of divinity; and the rather as the proofs of the being of a God, the creator, preserver, and supreme ruler of the universe, the author of all the relations of morality, and of the laws and obligations these infer, will be within the province of the professor of ethics; to which adding the developments of these moral obligations, of those in which all sects agree, with a knowledge of the languages, Hebrew, Greek, and Latin, a basis will be formed common to all sects. Proceeding thus far without offence to the Constitution, we have thought it proper at this point to leave every sect to provide, as they think fittest, the means of further instruction in their own peculiar tenets.

We are further of opinion, that after declaring by law that certain sciences shall be taught in the University, fixing the number of professors they require, which we think should, at present, be ten, limiting (except as to the professors who shall be first engaged in each branch,) a maximum for their salaries, (which should be a certain but moderate subsistence, to be made up by liberal tuition fees, as an excitement to assiduity), it will be best to leave to the discretion of the visitors, the grouping of these sciences together, according to the accidental qualifications of the professors; and the introduction also of other branches of science, when enabled by private donations, or by public provision, and called for by the increase of population, or other change of circumstances; to establish beginnings, in short, to be developed by time, as those who come after us shall find expedient. They will be more advanced than we are in science and in useful arts, and will know best what will suit the circumstances of their day.

We have proposed no formal provision for the gymnastics of the school, although a proper object of attention for every institution of youth. These exercises with ancient nations, constituted the principal part of the education of their youth. Their arms and mode of warfare rendered them severe in the extreme; ours, on the same correct principle, should be adapted to our arms and warfare; and the manual exercise, military manoeuvres, and tactics generally, should be the frequent exercise of the students, in their hours of recreation. It is at that age of aptness, docility, and emulation of the practices of manhood, that such things are soonest learnt and longest remembered. The use of tools too in the manual arts is worthy of encouragement, by facilitating to such as choose it, an admission into the neighboring workshops. To these should be added the arts which embellish life, dancing, music, and drawing; the last more especially, as an important part of military education. These innocent arts furnish amusement and happiness to those who, having time on their hands, might less inoffensively employ it. Needing, at the same time, no regular incorporation with the institution, they may be left to accessory teachers, who will be paid by the individuals employing them, the University only providing proper apartments for their exercise.

The fifth duty prescribed to the Commissioners, is to propose such general provisions as may be properly enacted by the Legislature, for the better organizing and governing the University.

In the education of youth, provision is to be made for, 1, tuition; 2, diet; 3, lodging; 4, government; and 5, honorary excitements. The first of these constitutes the proper functions of the professors; 2, the dieting of the students should be left to private boarding houses of their own choice, and at their own expense; to be regulated by the Visitors from time to time, the house only being provided by the University within its own precincts, and thereby of course subjected to the general regimen, moral or sumptuary, which they shall prescribe. 3. They should be lodged in dormitories, making a part of the general system of buildings. 4. The best mode of government for youth, in large collections, is certainly a desideratum not yet attained with us. It may be well questioned whether fear after a certain age, is a motive to which we should have ordinary recourse. The human character is susceptible of other incitements to correct conduct, more worthy of employ, and of better effect. Pride of character, laudable ambition, and moral dispositions are innate correctives of the indiscretions of that lively age; and when strengthened by habitual appeal and exercise, have a happier effect on future character than the degrading motive of fear. Hardening them to disgrace, to corporal punishments, and servile humiliations cannot be the best process for producing erect character. The affectionate deportment between father and son, offers in truth the best example for that of tutor and pupil; and the experience and practice of other countries, in this respect, may be worthy of enquiry and consideration with us. It will then be for the wisdom and discretion of the Visitors to devise and perfect a proper system of government, which, if it be founded in reason and comity, will be more likely to nourish in the minds of our youth the combined spirit of order and self-respect, so congenial with our political institutions, and so important to be woven into the American character. 5. What qualifications shall be required to entitle to entrance into the University, the arrangement of the days and hours of lecturing for the different schools, so as to facilitate to the students the circle of attendance on them; the establishment of periodical and public examinations, the premiums to be given for distinguished merit; whether honorary degrees shall be conferred, and by what appellations; whether the title to these shall depend on the time the candidate has been at the University, or, where nature has given a greater share of understanding, attention, and application; whether he shall not be allowed the advantages resulting from these endowments, with other minor items of government, we are of opinion should be entrusted to the Visitors; and the statute under which we act having provided for the appointment of these, we think they should moreover be charged with

The erection, preservation, and repair of the buildings, the care of the grounds and appurtenances, and of the interest of the University generally.

That they should have power to appoint a bursar, employ a proctor, and all other necessary agents.

To appoint and remove professors, two-thirds of the whole number of Visitors voting for the removal.

To prescribe their duties and the course of education, in conformity with the law.

To establish rules for the government and discipline of the students, not contrary to the laws of the land.

To regulate the tuition fees, and the rent of the dormitories they occupy.

To prescribe and control the duties and proceedings of all officers, servants, and others, with respect to the buildings, lands, appurtenances, and other property and interests of the University.

To draw from the literary fund such moneys as are by law charged on it for this institution; and in general

To direct and do all matters and things which, not being inconsistent with the laws of the land, to them shall seem most expedient for promoting the purposes of the said institution; which several functions they should be free to exercise in the form of by-laws, rules, resolutions, orders, instructions, or otherwise, as they should deem proper.

That they should have two stated meetings in the year, and occasional meetings at such times as they should appoint, or on a special call with such notice as themselves shall prescribe by a general rule; which meetings should be at the University, a majority of them constituting a quorum for business; and that on the death or resignation of a member, or on his removal by the President and Directors of the Literary Fund, or the Executive, or such other authority as the Legislature shall think best, such President and Directors, or the Executive, or other authority, shall appoint a successor.

That the said Visitors should appoint one of their own body to be Rector, and with him be a body corporate, under the style and title of the Rector and Visitors of the University of Virginia, with the right, as such, to use a common seal; that they should have capacity to plead and be impleaded in all courts of justice, and in all cases interesting to the University, which may be the subjects of legal cognizance and jurisdiction; which pleas should not abate by the determination of their office, but should stand revived in the name of their successors, and they should be capable in law and in trust for the University, of receiving subscriptions and donations, real and personal, as well from bodies corporate, or persons associated, as from private individuals.

And that the said Rector and Visitors should, at all times, conform to such laws as the Legislature may, from time to time, think proper to enact for their government; and the said University should, in all things, and at all times, be subject to the control of the Legislature.

And lastly, the Commissioners report to the Legislature the following conditional offers to the President and Directors of the Literary Fund, for the benefit of the University:

On the condition that Lexington, or its vicinity, shall be selected as the site of the University, and that the same be permanently established there within two years from the date, John Robinson, of Rockbridge county, has executed a deed to the President and Directors of the Literary Fund, to take effect at his death, for the following tracts of land, to wit:

400 acres on the North fork of James river, known by the name of Hart's bottom, purchased of the late Gen. Bowyer.

171 acres adjoining the same, purchased of James Griggsby.

203 acres joining the last mentioned tract, purchased of William Paxton.

112 acres lying on the North river, above the lands of Arthur Glasgow, conveyed to him by William Paxton's heirs.

500 acres adjoining the lands of Arthur Glasgow, Benjamin Camden and David Edmonson.

545 acres lying in Pryor's gap, conveyed to him by the heirs of William Paxton, deceased.

260 acres lying in Childer's gap, purchased of Wm. Mitchell.

300 acres lying, also, in Childer's gap, purchased of Nicholas Jones.

500 acres lying on Buffalo, joining the lands of Jas. Johnston.

340 acres on the Cowpasture river, conveyed to him by General James Breckenridge—reserving the right of selling the two last mentioned tracts, and converting them into other lands contiguous to Hart's bottom, for the benefit of the University; also, the whole of his slaves, amounting to 57 in number; one lot of 22 acres, joining the town of Lexington, to pass immediately on the establishment of the University, together with all the personal estate of every kind, subject only to the payment of his debts and fulfillment of his contracts.

It has not escaped the attention of the Commissioners, that the deed referred to is insufficient to pass the estate in the lands intended to be conveyed, and may be otherwise defective; but, if necessary, this defect may be remedied before the meeting of the Legislature, which the Commissioners are advised will be done.

The Board of Trustees of Washington College have also proposed to transfer the whole of their funds, viz: 100 shares in the funds of the James River Company, 31 acres of land upon which their buildings stand, their philosophical apparatus, their expected interest in the funds of the Cincinnati Society, the libraries of the Graham and Washington Societies, and $3,000 in cash, on condition that a reasonable provision be made for the present professors. A subscription has also been offered by the people of Lexington and its vicinity, amounting to $17,878, all which will appear from the deed and other documents, reference thereto being had.

In this case, also, it has not escaped the attention of the Commissioners, that questions may arise as to the power of the trustees to make the above transfers.

On the condition that the Central College shall be made the site of the University, its whole property, real and personal, in possession or in action, is offered. This consists of a parcel of land of 47 acres, whereon the buildings of the college are begun, one pavilion and its appendix of dormitories being already far advanced, and with one other pavilion, and equal annexation of dormitories, being expected to be completed during the present season—of another parcel of 153 acres, near the former, and including a considerable eminence very favorable for the erection of a future observatory; of the proceeds of the sales of two glebes, amounting to $3,280 86 cents; and of a subscription of $41,248, on papers in hand, besides what is on outstanding papers of unknown amount, not yet returned—out of these sums are to be taken, however, the cost of the lands, of the buildings, and other works done, and for existing contracts. For the conditional transfer of these to the President and Directors of the Literary Fund, a regular power, signed by the subscribers and founders of the Central College generally, has been given to its Visitors and Proctor, and a deed conveying the said property accordingly to the President and Directors of the Literary Fund, has been duly executed by the said Proctor, and acknowledged for record in the office of the clerk of the county court of Albemarle.

Signed and certified by the members present, each in his proper handwriting, this 4th day of August, 1818.

TH: JEFFERSON,	HUGH HOLMES,
CREED TAYLOR,	PHIL. C. PENDLETON,
PETER RANDOLPH,	SPENCER ROANE,
WM. BROCKENBROUGH,	JOHN M. C. TAYLOR,
ARCH'D RUTHERFORD,	J. G. JACKSON,
ARCH'D STUART,	PHIL. SLAUGHTER,
JAMES BRECKENRIDGE,	WM. H. CABELL,
HENRY E. WATKINS,	NAT. H. CLAIBORNE,
JAMES MADISON,	WM. A. C. DADE,
A. T. MASON,	WILLIAM JONES,

THOMAS WILSON.

APPENDIX XVIII

EXTRACT FROM A LETTER TO JOSEPH C. CABELL
FROM POPLAR FOREST, VIRGINIA, NOVEMBER 28, 1820

(Cabell, pp. 184–186)

I enclose you now a paper presenting some views which may be useful to you in conversations, to rebut exaggerated estimates of what our institution is to cost, and reproaches of deceptive estimates. $162,364 will be about the cost of the whole establishment when completed. Not an office at Washington has cost less. The single building of the courthouse of Henrico, has cost nearly that; and the massive walls of the millions of bricks of William & Mary, could not be now built for a greater sum.

Surely Governor Clinton's display of the gigantic efforts of New York towards the education of their citizens will stimulate the pride as well as the patriotism of our Legislature, to look to the reputation and safety of their own country, to rescue it from the degradation of becoming the Barbary of the Union, and of falling into the ranks of our own negroes. To that condition it is fast sinking. We shall be in the hands of the other States, what our indigenous predecessors were, when invaded by the science and arts of Europe. The mass of education in Virginia, before the revolution, placed her with the foremost of her sister colonies. What is her education now? Where is it? The little we have, we import, like beggars, from other States; or import their beggars to bestow on us their miserable crumbs. And what is wanting to restore us to our station among our confederates? Not more money from the people. Enough has been raised by them, and appropriated to this very object. It is that it should be employed understandingly, and for their greatest good. That good requires that, while they are instructed in general, competently to the common businesses of life, others should apply their genius with necessary information, to the useful arts, to inventions for saving labor, and increasing our comforts, to nourishing our health, to civil government, military science, &c.

Would it not have a good effect for the friends of the University, to take the lead in proposing and effectuating a practicable scheme of elementary schools? To assume the character of the friends, rather than the opponents, of that object? The present plan has appropriated to the primary schools $45,000 for three years, making $135,000. I should be glad to know if this sum has educated one hundred and thirty-five poor children? I doubt it much. And if it has, they have cost us $1,000 a piece, for what might have been done with $30. Supposing the literary revenue $60,000, I think it demonstrable that this sum equally divided between the two objects, would amply suffice for both. One hundred counties divided into about twelve wards each, on an average, and a school in each ward, of perhaps ten children, would be 1,200 schools, distributed proportionably over the surface of the State. The inhabitants of each ward, meeting together, (as when they work on the roads,) building good log-houses for their school and teacher, and contributing for his provisions, rations of pork, beef, and corn in the proportion, each of his other taxes, would thus lodge and feed him without feeling it, and those of them who are able, paying for the tuition of their own children, would leave no call on the public fund, but for the tuition fee of here and there an incidental pauper who would still be fed and lodged with his parents. Suppose this fee $10, and $300 apportioned to a county on an average, (more or less duly proportioned,) would there be thirty such paupers for every county? I think not. The truth is, that the want of common education with us is not from our poverty, but from the want of an orderly system. More money is now paid for the education of a part, than would be paid for that of the whole if systematically arranged. Six thousand common schools in New York, fifty pupils in each, 300,000 in all; $160,000 annually paid to the masters; forty established academies, with 2,218 pupils, and five colleges with 718 students; to which last classes of institutions $720,000 have been given; and the whole appropriations for education estimated at two and a half millions of dollars!

What a pigmy to this is Virginia become! With a population all but equal to that of New York! And whence this difference? From the difference their rulers set on the value of knowledge and the prosperity it produces. But still if a pigmy, let her do what a pigmy may do. If among fifty children in each of the six thousand schools of New York, there are only paupers enough to employ $25 of public money to each school, surely among the ten children of each of our 1,200 schools, the same sum of $25 to each school will teach its paupers, (five times as much as to the same numbers in New York,) and will amount for the whole to $30,000 a year, the one-half only of our literary revenue.

Do then, dear sir, think of this, and engage our friends to take in hand the whole subject. It will reconcile the friends of the elementary schools, (and none is more warmly so than myself,) lighten the difficulties of the University, and promote in every order of men the degree of instruction proportioned to their condition, and to their views in life. It will combine with the mass of our force, a wise direction of it, which will ensure to our country its future prosperity and safety. I had formerly thought that visitors for the schools might be chosen by the county, and charged to provide teachers for every ward, and to superintend them. I now think it would be better for every ward to choose its own resident visitor, whose business it would be to keep a teacher in the ward, to superintend the school, and to call meetings of the ward for all purposes relating to it; their accounts to be settled and wards laid off by the courts. I think ward elections better for many reasons, one of which is sufficient, that it will keep elementary education out of the hands of fanaticising preachers, who in county elections would be universally chosen, and the predominant sect of the county would possess itself of all its schools.

A wrist stiffened by an ancient accident, now more so by the effect of age, renders writing a slow and irksome operation with me. I cannot, therefore, present these views by separate letters, to each of our colleagues in the Legislature; but must pray you to communicate them to Mr. Johnson and General Breckenridge, and to request them to consider this as equally meant for them.

APPENDIX XIX

LETTER TO JOSEPH C. CABELL FROM MONTICELLO, JANUARY 31, 1821

(Cabell, p. 201)

DEAR SIR,—Your favors of the 18th and 25th came together, three days ago. They fill me with gloom as to the dispositions of our Legislature towards the University. I perceive that I am not to live to see it opened. As to what had better be done within the limits of their will, I trust with entire confidence to what yourself, General Breckenridge, and Mr. Johnson shall think best. You will see what is practicable, and give it such shape as you think best. If a loan is to be resorted to, I think $60,000 will be necessary, including the library. Its instalments cannot begin until those of the former loan are accomplished; and they should not begin later, nor be less than $13,000 a year. (I think it safe to retain $2,000 a year for the care of the buildings, improvement of the grounds, and unavoidable contingencies.) To extinguish this second loan, will require between five and six instalments, which will carry us to the end of 1833, or thirteen years from this time. My individual opinion is, that we had better not open the institution, until the buildings, library and all, are finished, and our funds cleared of incumbrance. These buildings, once erected, will secure the full object infallibly at the end of thirteen years, and as much earlier as an enlightened Legislature shall happen to come into place. And if we were to begin sooner, with half funds only, it would satisfy the common mind, prevent their aid beyond that point, and our institution remaining at that forever, would be no more than the paltry academies we now have. Even with the whole funds, we shall be reduced to six professors, while Harvard will still prime it over us, with her twenty professors. How many of our youths she now has, learning the lessons of Anti-Missourianism, I know not; but a gentleman lately from Princeton, told me he saw there the list of the students at that place, and that more than half were Virginians. These will return home, no doubt, deeply impressed with the sacred principles of our holy alliance of Restrictionists.

But the gloomiest of all prospects is in the desertion of the best friends of the institution; for desertion I must call it. I know not the necessities which may force this on you. General Cocke, you say, will explain them to me; but I cannot conceive them, nor persuade myself they are uncontrolable. I have ever hoped that yourself, General Breckenridge, and Mr. Johnson, would stand at your posts in the Legislature until every thing was effected, and the institution opened. If it is so difficult to get along with all the energy and influence of our present colleagues in the Legislature, how can we expect to proceed at all, reducing our moving power? I know well your devotion to your country, and your foresight of the awful scenes coming on her, sooner or later. With this foresight, what service can we ever render her equal to this? What object of our lives can we propose, so important? What interest of our own, which ought not to be postponed to this? Health, time, labor, on what in the single life which nature has given us, can these be better bestowed than on this immortal boon to our country? The exertions and the mortifications are temporary; the benefit eternal. If any member of our college of visitors could justifiably withdraw from this sacred duty, it would be myself, who, *"quadragenis stipendiis jamdudum peractis,"* have neither vigor of body nor mind left to keep the field. But I will die in the last ditch. And so, I hope, you will, my friend, as well as our firm-breasted brothers and colleagues, Mr. Johnson and General Breckenridge. Nature will not give you a second life wherein to atone for the omissions of this. Pray then, dear and very dear sir, do not think of deserting us; but view the sacrifices which seem to stand in your way, as the lesser duties, and such as ought to be postponed to this, the greatest of all. Continue with us in these holy labors, until having seen their accomplishment, we may say with old Simeon, *"nunc dimittis, Domine."* Under all circumstances, however, of praise or blame, I shall be affectionately yours.

Mr. Cabell.

TH: JEFFERSON

APPENDIX XX

EXTRACT FROM A LETTER TO GENERAL BRECKENRIDGE, FEBRUARY 15, 1821

(Honeywell, Appendix K, pp. 263–264)

DEAR SIR,

I learn with deep affliction, that nothing is likely to be done for our University this year. So near as it is to the shore that one shove more would land it there, I had hoped that would be given; and that we should open with the next year an institution on which the fortunes of our country depend more than may meet the general eye. The reflections that the boys of this age are to be the men of the next; that they should be prepared to receive the holy charge which we are cherishing to deliver over to them; that in establishing an institution of wisdom for them we secure it to all our future generations; that in fulfilling this duty we bring home to our own bosoms the sweet consolation of seeing our sons rising, under a luminous tuition, to destinies of high promise; these are considerations which will occur to all. But all, I fear, do not see the speck in our horizon which is to burst on us as a tornado, sooner or later. The line of division lately marked out between different portions of our confederacy, is such as will never, I fear, be obliterated, and we are now trusting to those who are against us in position and principle, to fashion to their own form the minds and affections of our youth. If, as has been estimated, we send 300,000. D. a year to the Northern seminaries for the instruction of our own sons, then we must have there at all times 500. of our sons imbiding opinions and principles in discord with those of their own country. This canker is eating on the vitals of our existence, and if not arrested at once will be beyond remedy. We are now certainly furnishing recruits to their school. If it be asked what are we to do? or said that we cannot give the last lift to the University without stopping our primary schools and these we think the most important; I answer, I know their importance. Nobody can doubt my zeal for the general instruction of the people. Who first started that idea I may surely say myself. Turn to the bill in the revised code which I drew more than 40. years ago; and before which the idea of a plan for the education of the people generally had never been suggested in this state. There you will see developed the first rudiments of the whole system of general education we are now urging and acting on. And it is well known to those with whom I have acted on this subject, that I never have proposed a sacrifice of the primary to the ultimate grade of instruction. Let us keep our eye steadily on the whole system. If we cannot do every thing at once, let us do one at a time. The primary schools need no preliminary expence. The ultimate grade requires a considerable expenditure in advance. A suspension of proceeding for a year or two on the primary schools, and an application of the whole income during that time, to the completion of the buildings necessary for the University, would enable us then to start both institutions at the same time. The intermediate branch of colleges, academies, and private classical schools, for the middle grade, may hereafter receive any necessary aids when the funds shall have become competent. In the mean time they are going on sufficiently, as they have ever yet gone on, at the private expence of those who use them, and who in numbers and means are competent to their own exigencies. The experience of 3. years has, I presume, left no doubt that the present plan of primary schools, of putting money into the hands of 1200. persons acting for nothing, and under no responsibility, is entirely inefficient. Some other must be thought of; and during this pause, if it be only for a year, the whole revenue of that year, with that of the last 3. years which has not been already thrown away, would place our University in readiness to start with a better organization of primary schools, and both may then go on, hand in hand, for ever. No diminution of the capital will in this way have been incurred; a principle which ought to be deemed sacred. A relinquishment of interest on the late loan of 60,000. D., would so far also forward the university, without lessening the capital. But what may be best done, I leave with entire confidence to yourself and your colleagues in legislation, who know better than I do the conditions of the literary fund, and its wisest application; and I shall acquiesce with perfect resignation to their will. I have brooded, perhaps with fondness, over this establishment, as it held up to me the hope of continuing to be useful while I continued to live. I had believed that the course and circumstances of my life had placed within my power some services favorable to the out-set of the institution. But this may be egoism; pardonable perhaps when I express a consciousness that my colleagues and successors will do as well, whatever the legislature shall enable them to do.

I have thus, my dear Sir, opened my bosom, with all it's anxieties, freely to you. I blame nobody, for seeing things in a different light. I am sure all act conscientiously, and that all will be done honestly and wisely which can be done. I yield the concerns of the world with cheerfulness to those who are appointed in the order of nature to succeed to them; and for yourself, for our colleagues, and for all in charge of our country's future fame and fortune, I offer up sincere prayers.

Th: Jefferson

Appendixes

APPENDIX XXI

EXTRACT FROM A LETTER TO JOSEPH C. CABELL
FROM MONTICELLO, DECEMBER 28, 1822

(Cabell, p. 260)

DEAR SIR,—Yours of the 19th was received some days ago; those of the 23d, the day before yesterday. At the same time with the former, I received one of the same date from Mr. Rives, proposing a question to me, which, as he is absent, I will answer to you. It was—if the remission of the principal debt, and an accommodation of the cost of the library cannot both be obtained, which would be most desirable? Without any question, the latter. Of all things the most important, is the completion of the buildings. The remission of the debt will come of itself. It is already remitted in the mind of every man, even of the enemies of the institution. And there is nothing pressing very immediately for its expression. The great object of our aim from the beginning, has been to make the establishment the most eminent in the United States, in order to draw to it the youth of every State, but especially of the south and west. We have proposed, therefore, to call to it characters of the first order of science from Europe, as well as our own country; and, not only by the salaries and the comforts of their situation, but by the distinguished scale of its structure and preparation, and the promise of future eminence which these would hold up, to induce them to commit their reputation to its future fortunes. Had we built a barn for a college, and log huts for accommodations, should we ever have had the assurance to propose to an European professor of that character to come to it? Why give up this important idea, when so near its accomplishment that a single lift more effects it? It is not a half project which is to fill up the enticement of character from abroad. To stop where we are, is to abandon our high hopes, and become suitors to Yale and Harvard for their secondary characters to become our first. Have we been laboring then merely to get up another Hampden Sidney or Lexington? Yet to this it sinks, if we abandon foreign aid. The report of Rockfish Gap, sanctioned by the Legislature, authorized us to aim at much higher things; and the abandonment of the enterprise where we are, would be a relinquishment of the great idea of the Legislature of 1818, and shrinking it into a country academy. The opening of the institution in a half-state of readiness, would be the most fatal step which could be adopted. It would be an impatience defeating its own object, by putting on a subordinate character in the outset, which never would be shaken off, instead of opening largely and in full system. Taking our stand on commanding ground at once, will beckon every thing to it, and a reputation once established, will maintain itself for ages. To secure this, a single sum of fifty or sixty thousands of dollars is wanting. If we cannot get it now, we will at another or another

144

trial. Courage and patience is the watchword. Delay is an evil, which will pass; despair loses all. Let us never give back. The thing will carry itself, and with firmness and perseverance we shall place our country on its high station, and we shall receive for it the blessings of posterity. I think your idea of a loan, and placing it on the sinking fund, an excellent one.

APPENDIX XXII

LETTER TO JEFFERSON FROM JOSEPH C. CABELL, RICHMOND, JANUARY 23, 1823

(Cabell, p. 268)

DEAR SIR,—Your favor of 13th instant came safely to hand by the mail. I have shewn it to Mr. Gordon and Mr. Rives. My own impression is, that in touching the subject of the unliquidated debt, we should merely guard against future unfavorable imputations, by stating that it might and probably would exceed the conjectural amount mentioned in your letter, and that when you wrote, the settlement was in a progressive state. The county delegates seem disposed to say nothing about it. I have referred the matter to their discretion. When the bill gets to the Senate, I shall say something on the subject.

In regard to the academies and primary schools, I think our most prudent course, at this time, is neither to enter into an alliance with them, nor to make war upon them. It would be difficult to imagine a state of things in regard to these other branches of the system more favorable to us than that which now exists. The funds are limited, and we wish to avoid a competitor. The colleges cannot all be gratified, and they will defeat one another. The primary schools are in a state of discredit, and the public mind is not now disposed to increase the appropriation to them. If we amend the system at this time, and give it credit and honor, this ally will become our worst enemy. The popular branch of the system would swallow up all the funds. Even now an effort will be made to divide with us in every appropriation; but the discredit into which the popular branch has fallen, will defeat the measure.

Besides, there are great intrinsic difficulties in the subject. When your bill was brought in some years ago by Mr. Taylor, of Chesterfield, I consulted all the best heads of my acquaintance then about the Seat of Government, and every effort was made to smooth away the difficulties of the subject; and though many plans were suggested, none met with general approbation. At some future time, I would cheerfully enter again on this difficult and thorny question. I think we would do well to decline it at this time, and take advantage of the favorable breeze that now wafts us along.

I have imparted these views to Mr. Rives, and left him to pursue his own course. Mr. Gordon concurs with me. Mr. Rives did not propose to move the subject of the primary schools till the Loan Bill should be acted on. But the bonds will remain to be cancelled, and the objections would continue till the University should get into operation. I have thought, and still think, that we should act with good faith to the primary schools; but *that* would dictate merely that we should not attempt to take from them any of the $45,000, till experience and public opinion demand the measure. I have attempted, in the county where I reside, to exhibit proofs of my real desire to give that system a fair trial. Our proceedings were printed and distributed over the State. But, last year, I saw more clearly than ever the inherent defects of that system. It will require great alteration and amendment. But for us to move in it, I think, the time has not arrived.

As to the colleges and academies, I differ from some of our friends. I would vote for an appropriation to Hampden Sidney, and not wait till the funds shall be sufficient for the whole corps of colleges. I think some aid to that college would now be useful and well-timed. However, on this subject, as on that of the question of removing the Seat of Government, I think we should not discover the zeal of partizans. Politeness to all, interference with none, and devotion to our object, constitute the policy that ought, in my opinion, to govern the course of the friends of the University at this time.

You must be surprised at the slow progress of our bill. The tardiness of its movement is to be regretted. But I do not know how it could be avoided. If it had been called up out of its regular turn, perhaps the irregularity of the course might give rise to animadversions. It will be read, in its turn, for the first time, to-day or to-morrow. It went through the committee without opposition. It will doubtless be opposed in the House, but from every thing I can learn I think there cannot be much doubt of its success. Should it pass late in the session, I should hope that a meeting on the 1st Monday in April might answer the purposes of the institution. There could be no doubt of the confirmation of the loan by the board, and the delay would probably throw the loss of interest on the literary fund, and save so much to the University.

I am, dear sir,

Ever faithfully, your friend,

JOSEPH C. CABELL.

Mr. Jefferson.

APPENDIX XXIII

LETTER TO JOSEPH C. CABELL FROM JEFFERSON, MONTICELLO, JANUARY 28, 1823

(Cabell, p. 269)

DEAR SIR,—I have received your favor of the 23d, and it has entirely converted me to your opinion that we should let the primary schools lie for the present, avail ourselves of their temporary descredit, and of the breeze in our favor, until the University is entirely secured in the completion of its buildings and remission of its debt; and then to come forward heartily, as the patrons of the primaries, on some plan which will allow us a fairer share of the common fund. Our present portion would enable us to have put six professors, whereas the law contemplates ten, which number is really necessary, and would require at least $10,000 additional to our present annuity. I have accordingly written to Mr. Rives to retract the opinion I had expressed to him in favor of immediately taking up the subject of remodelling those schools. But I still differ from you as to giving a dollar to Hampden Sidney. Let this, with all the other intermediate academies, be taken up in their turn and provided for systematically and proportionally. To give to that singly, will be a departure from principle, will make the others our enemies, and is not necessary. The University is advanced to that point, from which it must and will carry itself through; and it will strengthen daily. In the mean time we need take no part for or against either the academies or schools. If, after the passage of the bill for the loan, the remission of the whole debt can be obtained without difficulty at the present session, it would have the effect of enabling us at once to take measures for engaging professors, and for opening the institution at the end of the year, which a postponement to the next session would delay another year.

You supposed that our April meeting will be early enough for acting on the law to be passed. The only thing pressing will be the engaging our workmen. If Mr. Johnson, Mr. Loyall, and yourself should advise me, by letter, that you approve of the acceptance of the loan, I will take measures to get the same opinion from the other three gentlemen, and shall not scruple to engage the workmen, and to have preparations for bricks commenced. We can do without the money till the April meeting. If this opinion be given as soon as the bill passes the Lower House, I presume we may act immediately, without fearing a veto from the Senate. I salute you with cordial affection and respect.

TH: JEFFERSON.

Mr. Cabell.

APPENDIX XXIV

EXTRACT FROM A LETTER TO GEORGE TICKNOR
FROM MONTICELLO, JULY 16, 1823

(Lipscomb, vol. XV, pp. 455–456)

DEAR SIR,—I received in due time your favor of June 16th, and with it your syllabus of lectures on Spanish literature. I have considered this with great interest and satisfaction, as it gives me a model of course I wish to see pursued in the different branches of instruction in our University; i.e., a methodical, critical, and profound explanation by way of protection of every science we propose to teach. I am not fully informed of the practices at Harvard, but there is one from which we shall certainly vary, although it has been copied, I believe, by nearly every college and academy in the United

States. That is, the holding the students all to one prescribed course of reading, and disallowing exclusive application to those branches only which are to qualify them for the particular vocations to which they are destined. We shall, on the contrary, allow them uncontrolled choice in the lectures they shall choose to attend, and require elementary qualification only, and sufficient age. Our institution will proceed on the principle of doing all the good it can without consulting its own pride or ambition; of letting every one come and listen to whatever he thinks may improve the condition of his mind. The rock which I most dread is the discipline of the institution, and it is that on which most of our public schools labor. The insubordination of our youth is now the greatest obstacle to their education. We may lessen the difficulty, perhaps, by avoiding too much government, by requiring no useless observances, none which shall merely multiply occasions for dissatisfaction, disobedience and revolt by referring to the more discreet of themselves the minor discipline, the graver to the civil magistrates, as in Edinburgh. On this head I am anxious for information of the practices of other places, having myself had little experience of the government of youth. I presume there are printed codes of the rules of Harvard, and if so, you would oblige me by sending me a copy, and of those of any other academy which you think can furnish anything useful. You flatter me with a visit "as soon as you learn that the University is fairly opened." A visit from you at any time will be the most welcome possible to all our family, who remember with peculiar satisfaction the pleasure they received from your former one. But were I allowed to name the time, it should not be deferred beyond the autumn of the ensuing year. Our last building, and that which will be the principal ornament and keystone, giving unity to the whole, will then be nearly finished, and afford you a gratification compensating the trouble of the journey. We shall then, also, be engaged in our code of regulations preparatory to our opening, which may, perhaps, take place in the beginning of 1825. There is no person from whose information of the European institutions, and especially their discipline, I should expect so much aid in that difficult work. Come, then, dear Sir, at that, or any earlier epoch, and give to our institution the benefit of your counsel. I know that you scout, as I do, the idea of any rivalship. Our views are catholic for the improvement of our country by science, and indeed, it is better even for your own University to have its yokemate at this distance, rather than to force a nearer one from the increasing necessity for it. And how long before we may expect others in the southern, western, and middle region of this vast country?

Appendixes

APPENDIX XXV

In the early times of the colony, when lands were to be obtained for little or nothing, some provident individuals procured large grants; and, desirous of founding great families for themselves, settled them on their descendants in fee tail. The transmission of this property from generation to generation, in the same name, raised up a distinct set of families, who, being privileged by law in the perpetuation of their wealth, were thus formed into a Patrician order, distinguished by the splendor and luxury of their establishments. From this order, too, the king habitually selected his counsellors of State; the hope of which distinction devoted the whole corps to the interests and will of the crown. To annul this privilege, and instead of an aristocracy of wealth, of more harm and danger, than benefit, to society, to make an opening for the aristocracy of virtue and talent, which nature has wisely provided for the direction of the interests of society, and scattered with equal hand through all its conditions, was deemed essential to a well-ordered republic. To effect it, no violence was necessary, no deprivation of natural right, but rather an enlargement of it by a repeal of the law. For this would authorize the present holder to divide the property among his children equally, as his affections were divided; and would place them, by natural generation, on the level of their fellow citizens. But this repeal was strongly opposed by Mr. Pendleton, who was zealously attached to ancient establishments; and who, taken all in all, was the ablest man in debate I have ever met with.

The acts of Assembly concerning the College of William and Mary, were properly within Mr. Pendleton's portion of our work; but these related chiefly to its revenue, while its constitution, organization and scope of science, were derived from its charter. We thought that on this subject, a systematical plan of general education should be proposed, and I was requested to undertake it. I accordingly prepared three bills for the Revisal, proposing three distinct grades of education, reaching all classes. 1st. Elementary schools, for all children generally, rich and poor. 2d. Colleges, for a middle degree of instruction, calculated for the common purposes of life, and such as would be desirable for all who were in easy circumstances. And, 3d, an ultimate grade for teaching the sciences generally, and in their highest degree. The first bill proposed to lay off every county into Hundreds, or Wards, of a proper size and population for a school, in which reading, writing, and common arithmetic should be taught; and that the whole State should be divided into twenty-four districts, in each of which should be a school for classical learning, grammar, geography, and the higher branches of numerical arithmetic. The second bill proposed to amend the constitution of William and Mary College, to enlarge its sphere of science, and to make it in fact a University. The third was for the establishment of a library. These bills were not acted on until the same year, '96, and then only so much of the first as provided for elementary schools. The College of William and Mary was an establishment purely of the Church of England; the Visitors were required to be all of that Church; the Professors to subscribe its thirty-nine Articles; its Students to learn its Catechism; and one of its fundamental objects was declared to be, to raise up Ministers for that church. The religious jealousies, therefore, of all the dissenters, took alarm lest this might give an ascendancy to the Anglican sect, and refused acting on that bill. Its local eccentricity, too, and unhealthy autumnal climate, lessened the general inclination towards it. And in the Elementary bill, they inserted a provision which completely defeated it; for they left it to the court of each county to determine for itself, when this act should be carried into execution, within their county. One provision of the bill was, that the expenses of these schools should be borne by the inhabitants of the county, every one in proportion to his general tax rate. This would throw on wealth the education of the poor; and the justices, being generally of the more wealthy class, were unwilling to incur that burden, and I believe it was not suffered to commence in a single county. I shall recur again to this subject, towards the close of my story, if I should have life and resolution enough to reach that term; for I am already tired of talking about myself.

The bill on the subject of slaves, was a mere digest of the existing laws respecting them, without any intimation of a plan for a future and general emancipation. It was thought better that this should be kept back, and attempted only by way of amendment, whenever the bill should be brought on. The principles of the amendment, however, were agreed on, that is to say, the freedom of all born after a certain day, and deportation at a proper age. But it was found that the public mind would not yet bear the proposition, nor will it bear it even at this day. Yet the day is not distant when it must bear and adopt it, or worse will follow. Nothing is more certainly written in the book of fate, than that these people are to be free; nor is it less certain that the two races, equally free, cannot live in the same government. Nature, habit, opinion have drawn indelible lines of distinction between them. It is still in our power to direct the process of emancipation and deportation, peaceably, and in such slow degree, as that the evil will wear off insensibly, and their place be, *pari passu,* filled up by free white laborers. If, on the contrary, it is left to force itself on, human nature must shudder at the prospect held up. We should in vain look for an example in the Spanish deportation or deletion of the Moors. This precedent would fall far short of our case.

I considered four of these bills, passed or reported, as forming a system by which every fibre would be eradicated of ancient or future aristocracy; and a foundation laid for a government truly republican. The repeal of the laws of entail would prevent the accumulation and perpetuation of wealth, in select families, and preserve the soil of the country from being daily more and more absorbed in mortmain. The abolition of primogeniture, and equal partition of inheritances, removed the feudal and unnatural distinctions which made one member of every family rich, and all the rest poor, substituting equal partition, the best of all Agrarian laws. The restoration of the rights of conscience relieved the people from taxation for the support of a religion not theirs; for the establishment was truly of the religion of the rich, the dissenting sects being entirely composed of the less wealthy people; and these, by the bill for a general education, would be qualified to understand their rights, to maintain them, and to exercise with intelligence their parts in self-government; and all this would be effected, without the violation of a single natural right of any one individual citizen. To these, too, might be added, as a further security, the introduction of the trial by jury, into the Chancery courts, which have already ingulfed, and continue to ingulf, so great a portion of the jurisdiction over our property.

APPENDIX XXVI

CHARLES F. MERCER'S BILL FOR A SYSTEM OF PUBLIC EDUCATION

The bill was passed by the Virginia House of Delegates but defeated in the Senate by a tie vote on February 20, 1817. In presenting this text in the appendix to his long address at Princeton in 1826, Mercer wrote that the bill "left the house of delegates very nearly in the subjoined form: the only material change having been effected with the opprobation of the mover,—by leaving the whole territory of the state open for the site of the University of Virginia." The text which follows is from the Appendix to Charles F. Mercer, *A Discourse on Popular Education* (Princeton, N. J.: Princeton Press, 1826).

I. *Be it enacted by the General Assembly,* That for the purpose of digesting and carrying into effect the system of public education provided for by the last general assembly, and recommended by the president and directors of the literary fund, there shall be elected *annually* by joint ballot of the senate and house of delegates *ten* directors, who shall be styled "The board of public instruction," in which name they shall have a common seal and perpetual succession; shall be capable of suing and being sued, pleading and being impleaded, and shall have and enjoy all the rights and privileges of a corporation.

II. *And be it further enacted,* That the governor of the commonwealth shall be, *ex officio,* president of "The board of public instruction"; that any citizen of this commonwealth shall be capable of being a director of the board, but that *two* of the whole number of the directors shall reside westward of the Allegany mountains; two between the Allegany and the Blue Ridge, *four* between the Blue Ridge, and the great post road, which passing through the territory of the commonwealth, crosses the principal rivers thereof at or about the head of tide water; and the residue between that road and the sea coast. The board shall annually elect from their own body a vice-president, who, in the absence of the president, shall preside over their deliberations; they shall have power also to appoint a secretary, and such officers as may be required for conducting the business of the board, who shall receive for their services such compensation as the board may allow to be paid out of the revenue of the literary fund. Each director of the board shall receive, from the same fund, such compensation for his services as may be allowed by law, which, until otherwise provided, shall be the same mileage for travelling to and from the place of sitting, and the same pay, per diem, during his necessary attendance on the board, as is now allowed by law to a member of the general assembly. A majority of the whole number of directors shall be necessary to constitute a board for the transaction of business, but the president or a single director may adjourn from day to day, until a board is formed. The board shall have power to fill any vacancy which may occur in their own body, either from death, resignation, removal, inability, or any other cause; they shall hold an annual meeting at   or at such other place as may be designated by law, until the university of Virginia shall be erected, after which, their annual meetings shall be held thereat. Their first annual meeting shall commence on the   and continue until the business of the board is transacted. At this meeting the board shall prescribe the time of their future annual meetings: but the president of the board may at his own pleasure, or shall at the request of any three directors thereof, convene an extra meeting of the board, for the transaction of any extraordinary business which may devolve on the corporation.

III. *And be it further enacted,* That the board may at any time enact, alter, or amend such rules, as to them may seem proper, for the purpose of regulating the order of their proceedings; they may adjourn for any period, or when occasion may require it, to meet at any other place, than that designated by law: they shall have power, subject to the limitations hereinafter provided, to establish and locate an university, to be called the university of Virginia; and the several colleges and academies hereinafter named or described; to determine the number and title of the professorships therein; to examine, appoint, and regulate the compensation of the several professors; to appoint the trustees of the several colleges and academies; to prescribe the course of instruction and discipline of the university, colleges, academies and primary schools; to provide some just and practical mode of advancing, from the primary schools to the academies, from the academies to the colleges, and from these to the university, as many of the most meritorious children of indigence, as the revenue of the literary fund may suffice to educate and maintain, after the whole system of public instruction, which the board may devise, shall have been put in operation. In framing this system, the board shall regard the primary schools as its foundation; and in its gradual execution, care shall be taken by the board of public instruction and by the president and directors of the literary fund, that no money shall be drawn from the revenue of that fund, for the establishment of the university, or any academy, or college, so long as it is probable that such an application of the fund may leave any primary schools unprovided for. In fine, the board of public instruction shall have power to enact, repeal, alter, or amend such by laws, rules and regulations relative to the various objects committed to their trust, as to them may seem expedient; provided the same be not inconsistent with the constitution and laws of Virginia or of the United States of America; and they are further authorized to recommend to the general assembly, from time to time, such general laws, in relation to public education, as may be calculated, in their opinion, to promote the intellectual and moral improvement of the commonwealth.

IV. *And be it further enacted,* That there shall be established within the commonwealth as many primary schools as shall tend to promote the easy diffusion of knowledge among the youth of all classes of society, and for establishing and properly regulating such schools, the whole territory of the commonwealth shall be divided into small and convenient jurisdictions to be denominated townships and wards. For this purpose the several county and corporation courts shall, at their next *May or June* term, appoint three commissioners, with authority to divide their respective counties into two or more townships and their respective corporations into two or more wards; provided, that no township shall contain fewer than *thirty* square miles, that where any city, borough or town, does not contain more than *one hundred* white families, it shall be comprehended in some township; where its population exceeds that number and does not reach *two* hundred white families, it shall constitute one ward; and where its population exceeds the number last mentioned, it may be divided into two or more wards, according to the discretion of the commissioners. The commissioners shall give separate denominations to each township and ward, so as to distinguish them from each other by name; and shall designate some central or convenient place in each, for the public meetings required to be held therein. They shall derive the boundaries of their townships and wards, from their county or corporation lines; and the mountains, streams of water, roads or streets intersecting their counties or corporations without regard to straight lines, and having described their townships or wards intelligibly, in writing, shall report them to their respective county or corporation courts. In performing this duty, the commissioners shall assemble at the seat of justice, in their respective counties or corporations; and shall receive, each, the sum of *two* dollars for every day not exceeding *three* in number, during which they may be so engaged in the public service. They shall sign and deliver their report, when finished, to the clerk of their county or corporation court; who shall certify the report to the court and the number of days employed by each commissioner in preparing the said report. Such certificate shall entitle the commissioner to receive such sum as it may specify, out of the ensuing county levy, and the court shall regulate the county levy, so as to provide therefor. As soon as the court shall receive the report, they shall attentively examine the same, and after making such corrections or alterations therein as they may deem necessary or expedient, they shall cause the clerk to insert the report, with the corrections or alterations if any have been made, in the record of their proceeding; and the said report, so recorded, shall be deemed and taken to be complete; *Provided,* That the court may, in the same manner, at any time thereafter, alter the boundary of any townships or ward: or increase the number of townships, or wards within their respective jurisdictions.

V. *And be it further enacted,* That whenever any person or persons, body politic or corporate, in any township or ward, shall provide a lot of ground of *two* acres in extent, or of the value of *two hundred* dollars, with a schoolhouse thereupon of the value of *two hundred and fifty* dollars, and convey the same to the president and directors of the literary fund, and have the conveyance therefor recorded in the proper court, and transmit a certified copy thereof to the said president and directors, said house shall be regarded as a primary school-house. The value or extent of the lot and house above mentioned to be ascertained by any three freeholders to be appointed by any magistrate residing in a neighbouring township or ward, and the valuation when made to be certified by a majority of the said freeholders to the president and directors of the literary fund.

VI. *And be it further enacted,* That whenever one or more primary schoolhouses shall have been provided, in manner aforesaid in any township or ward, the court of the county or corporation containing such township or ward, shall appoint three or more discreet persons, residing within the same, to hold an election therein, of five trustees for the government of such primary school, and of all other similar schools which may be at any time thereafter established within the limits of such township or ward. The commissioners so appointed shall give us public notice as practicable, of the time of holding the election, which shall be in not less than *thirty,* nor more than *sixty* days after their appointment. The place of holding such election shall be that designated for all public meetings within the township or ward. The mode of election shall be *viva voce,* and shall correspond, as nearly as possible, in all respects, with that of the delegates to the General Assembly. The polls shall be opened at ten o'clock in the morning of the day of election, and closed at sunset, or sooner if there be no opposition. All free white male housekeepers within the township or ward, shall have the right of suffrage. And when the polls shall have been closed, the commissioners shall proclaim the five persons having the greatest number of votes polled, to be duly elected trustees for one year, or until the next election of the primary schools of the township or ward for which the election shall have been held: and they shall certify to the court of the county or corporation, the names of the trustees so elected, the number of votes given for each, and the date of the election; which certificate shall be recorded by the clerk. Every election after the first, in any township or ward, shall be held on the *first Monday of May,* under the direction of commissioners appointed as aforesaid; but should the election fail for any cause, to be made on the day appointed, the trustees in office, for the past, shall serve for the ensuing year; and until their successors shall be elected in manner aforesaid. The trustees shall have power to fill any vacancy which may occur in their own body, either from death, resignation, removal, inability, or other causes. They shall have power to elect one of their body president thereof, who with any two others may constitute a board for transacting all necessary business devolving on the trustees of the primary schools of the township or ward. Their first meeting shall be held where their election was held; every other meeting at such place as the board of trustees may from time to time prescribe.

VII. *And be it further enacted,* That the board of trustees of the primary schools of any township or ward, shall have power to appoint a teacher for each of the primary schools within their respective townships or wards; to fix his salary; and to remove or displace him for incapacity or misconduct. They shall have authority to prescribe such rules and regulations relative to the instruction and discipline of their schools as may seem to them expedient, so that they be not inconsistent with the constitution and laws of the state, or of the United States, or of such general rules as the board of public instruction may prescribe, in relation to the government of the primary schools of the commonwealth.

VIII. *And be it further enacted,* That all the free white children resident within the township or ward in which any primary school is established, or where there is more than one such school within the township or ward, resident within the precincts laid down by the trustees for any particular school, shall be entitled to receive tuition at such school free of any charge whatever: *Provided,* That the board of trustees who have the government of the school may demand of such parents, guardians, or masters as are able to pay without inconvenience for the education of their children, wards, or apprentices, such fees of tuition as the said trustees may deem reasonable and proper: the fees to be made payable to, and to be collected by such person as the board of trustees may appoint, and to constitute a fund for the payment of a part of the salary of the teacher, and to purchase such books as may be necessary for the instruction of those children who are admitted into the school without any charge for tuition.

IX. *And be it further enacted,* That so soon as the board of trustees of the primary schools of any township or ward shall have appointed a teacher for any primary school, the president and directors of the Literary Fund shall have authority, and are required, on receiving notice thereof, to allot out of the annual revenue of the Literary Fund, *two hundred dollars* for the salary of such teacher, and *ten dollars* for the purchase of books and other implements of instruction, to be distributed, by order of the trustees, among those pupils of the school who are admitted therein free of charge, or who most need such provision. The salary of the teacher and the sum aforesaid shall be paid quarterly, by the president and directors of the Literary Fund, to the order of the board of trustees, subscribed by the president thereof, in behalf of the board, and countersigned by the clerk of the county court, who shall certify by endorsement thereon, that the president appears of record to be a trustee of the board elected for the said township or ward.

X. *And be it further enacted,* That the board of public instruction shall, as soon as can be conveniently done, divide the territory of the commonwealth, from reference to the last census of the free white population thereof, into   academical districts, containing each one or more counties, and as near as practicable, an equal number of such population, and cause their secretary to record such partition, having first numbered the districts therein from one upwards, in the minutes of their proceedings, and to transmit a certified copy thereof to the president and directors of the Literary Fund, who shall cause the same to be, in like manner, recorded; and shall also publish it in one or more newspapers printed in the city of Richmond, for the information of the people of the commonwealth.

XI. *And be it further enacted,* That where there shall exist in any such

155

district, an academy already established by law or otherwise, the trustees or other persons in whom the property of the same is vested, are authorized to submit to the board of public instruction a report of the actual condition of their institution; in which they shall set forth its relative position to the boundaries of the district, the number and dimensions, value and state of repair of the edifices belonging to it; and the extent of the ground on which they are erected; the number and denomination of the professors and teachers employed therein, and of the pupils educated thereat, in the year next preceding the date of the report: and should it be the opinion of the board, that such academy is properly situated for the benefit of the district, and that its buildings and grounds will answer their intended purposes, they may report their decision thereupon to the president and directors of the literary fund: and upon legal conveyance being made of the said ground and edifices to the said president and directors for the use of the literary fund, the said academy shall be entitled to all the benefits which may be extended to any academy which may be erected in pursuance of this act, and shall be subject to all the rules and regulations in relation to the government thereof, which the board of public instruction or the general assembly may provide for the general government of the academies of the commonwealth: *Provided,* That the trustees of any such academy shall continue to hold their offices and to supply vacancies occurring in their own body as heretofore authorized by law.

XII. *And be it further enacted,* That in case any such academy shall be chargeable with any existing debt, not exceeding one-fourth part in amount, of the actual value of its land and buildings; or the said buildings shall require repairs, or any enlargement or alteration thereof, the board of public instruction may recommend to the president and directors of the literary fund, an appropriation from any surplus revenue which may remain of the fund after providing for the several primary schools chargeable thereon, of a sum sufficient to discharge such debt, or to repair, alter, or enlarge the said buildings, so that such sum shall, in no case, exceed one fourth of the total value of such buildings, and of the ground on which they stand. Such sum the president and directors shall have power to pay, on the recommendation of the board, to any agent of the trustees of the said academy, who may be legally authorized by them to receive the same, the said agent executing his bond to the president and directors, with approved security, to apply the sum aforesaid to the purpose recommended by the board of public instruction.

XIII. *And be it further enacted,* That where, in any academical district, there shall be no academy in existence, or none which the board of public instruction may deem it proper to recommend to the president and directors of the literary fund, the board may accept a lot of ground of sufficient extent in their estimation, and conveniently situated in the district for the erection of an academy for the said district: *Provided,* That along with the lot of ground there shall be subscribed, by one or more persons, bodies politic or corporate, or the payment thereof be otherwise assured, to the president and directors of the literary fund, three-fourths of the sum necessary to erect suitable buildings thereon for such academy, which sum shall in no case be computed at less than *ten* thousand dollars: and upon a legal conveyance of the said lot of ground being accepted by the president and directors of the literary fund, and their being fully assured of the payment of the sum of money aforesaid, of which they shall give information in convenient time to the board of public instruction, the board shall appoint thirteen persons residing within the said district, trustees of the academy to be erected; who shall thenceforth be deemed a body corporate, by such title as the board of public instruction may prescribe; shall have authority to elect a president and vice president from their own body, and to fill all vacancies subsequently occurring therein from death, resignation, removal from the district, inability, or any other cause; shall have authority to provide a common seal; may sue and be sued, plead and be impleaded; and shall have and enjoy all the rights and privileges of a body politic in law. They may make, alter or amend such by-laws, rules and regulations as they shall deem necessary or expedient for the government of their own body, and of the professors, teachings and pupils of the academy of which they have charge: *Provided,* The same be not inconsistent with the constitution and laws of this state or of the United States, nor with such general regulations as the board of public instruction may provide for the general government of the academies of the commonwealth. They shall, as speedily as possible, provide by contact or otherwise, for the erection of the necessary edifices for their academy, and shall appoint an agent who shall have authority to collect the several sums subscribed thereto, and shall be entitled to receive in virtue of their order upon the president and directors of the literary fund, from the unappropriated revenue of that fund, a sum equivalent to one third of the whole amount actually paid by the subscribers towards the erection of the said buildings, to be applied by the trustees to the same object in aid of the subscription aforesaid.

XIV. *And be it further enacted,* That so soon as any academy is ready for the admission of pupils, the trustees of the same may recommend to the board of public instruction any person to be a professor or teacher therein, who if approved after examination in some mode to be provided by the board shall thenceforth be regarded as a professor or teacher of such Academy, but subject to removal at the pleasure of the trustees thereof for incapacity or misconduct, or in conformity with such contract as they may make with him for his services. Any vacancy occurring from any cause among the teachers of any such Academy shall be in like manner, filled; *Provided,* That during the recess of the Board of Public Instruction, the trustees may make a temporary appointment, to be confirmed or disapproved by the Board at their next session.

XV. *And be it further enacted,* That the trustees of any academy shall have power to fix the salaries of their respective teachers, subject to the control of the Board of Public Instruction; and when any such salary shall have been fixed, the professor or teacher entitled thereto shall receive one fourth of the annual amount thereof from the president and directors of the Literary Fund, to be paid quarter yearly out of such portion of the revenue of the said Fund, as shall not be required by the claims of any primary school, at the order of the board of trustees of the academy, subscribed by the president thereof in behalf of the board.

XVI. *And be it further enacted,* That upon the preceding conditions relative to the admission of existing academies into the system of public instruction hereby created, or to the creation of new academies as part of such system, the Board of Public Instruction and the president and directors of the Literary Fund are authorized to accept the Anne Smith Academy for the education of females, and to provide for the erection of one or more similar institutions, provided that the whole number within the Commonwealth shall not exceed three.

XVII. *And be it further enacted,* That the Board of Public Instruction shall have authority to establish within the Commonwealth three additional colleges to be denominated respectively, Pendleton, Wythe and Henry: the two first shall be located to the west of the Allegany mountain, one whereof shall be placed to the north and the other to the south of the dividing ridges of mountains which separate the head waters of the Little Kanawha and Monongalia rivers from those of the rivers Greenbrier and the Great Kanawha; and the third shall be established in some one of the following counties, below the Blue Ridge, viz. Madison, Culpepper, Fauquier, Prince William or Loudoun.

XVIII. In determining on the position of any of the said colleges, the board shall take into consideration, along with a due regard to the health, plenty, and economy or cheapness of living of the county in which such college is proposed to be established, the sums of money, tracts or parcels of land or other property in possession or reversion which any individual or individuals, body politic or corporate, may actually subscribe in favour of any particular site therefor: and no place shall be selected by the board for any such purpose until a lot of twenty-five acres of ground shall have been offered, and the sum of thirty thousand dollars shall have been subscribed for the purpose of erecting a college thereupon, and the sum of five thousand dollars for the purchase of a library and apparatus for the endowment of such college, when the edifices thereof shall have been erected.

XIX. *And be it further enacted,* That so soon as the Board of Public Instruction shall have agreed upon a proper site for any one of the colleges aforesaid, they shall design proper plans for the structure thereof and they shall appoint twenty-five trustees of such college, who shall, at their first meeting, elect a president and vice-president from their own body and thereafter be styled the president and trustees of the college of Pendleton, Wythe, or Henry (as the case be) in which name, they shall have a common seal, and perpetual succession: shall be capable of suing and being sued, pleading and being impleaded, and shall have and enjoy all the rights and privileges of a corporation. A majority of the said trustees shall constitute a board for the transaction of business and shall have every power in relation to their own proceedings, to the erection of the public edifices of their respective colleges, the appointment and removal of their professors and teachers, and the instruction and discipline of the students of such college as the trustees of the several academies aforesaid are empowered to exercise in relation to their respective academies, and to make such rules and regulations relative to all or any of these subjects as may seem to them expedient; provided they are not inconsistent with the constitution and laws of this State or of the United States, nor with such general regulations as the Board of Public Instruction may provide for the general government of the several colleges of this Commonwealth.

XX. *And be it further enacted,* That as soon as the president and directors of the Literary Fund shall have received a legal conveyance of the tract or parcel of land on which the said college is about to be erected, they shall have authority, and are required to subscribe towards the erection of the necessary buildings thereupon, a sum equivalent to one fourth of that otherwise subscribed as aforesaid, to be paid out of such part of the revenue of the Literary Fund, as shall remain, after providing for the primary schools and academies aforesaid, upon condition that of the sum so subscribed, the said president and directors shall pay no greater proportion at any time than shall have been actually paid, by the other subscribers thereto of the whole sum by them subscribed in money. All sums called for in virtue of any such subscription, shall be paid to the order of the board of trustees of any such college, subscribed by the president of the board in behalf thereof.

XXI. *And be it further enacted,* That at the like periods and upon the like evidence with those provided by the   section of this act for the salaries of the professors or teachers of any academy, the President and Directors of the Literary Fund shall pay out of the unappropriated revenue of the fund, one fifth part of the salaries of the professors and teachers of such college.

XXII. *And be it further enacted,* That in like manner and under like provisions in all respects the other colleges provided for by this act shall be established.

XXIII. *And be it further enacted,* That the Board of Public Instruction shall have authority to receive from the trustees or visitors of the existing colleges of William and Mary, Hampden Sydney, and Washington, any proposals which they may deem it proper to submit to the Board, for the purpose of having their respective institutions embraced within the system of public education to be created by this act: and in the event of such agreement being made between the trustees, or visitors of any one or all of the said colleges and the Board of Public Instruction, the former shall be entitled to the same provision for their respective professors and teachers which this act assures to the professors and teachers of the colleges to be created in pursuance thereof.

XXIV. The Board of Public Instruction shall, as soon as practicable, fix upon a proper site for the University of Virginia, in determining which, the Board shall take into consideration along with all those circumstances which appertain to the location of the several colleges aforesaid, the relation of the University to the geographical centre of the Commonwealth and to the principal channels of intercourse through its territory. They shall locate the University therefore at some place between the Blue Ridge and Allegany mountains, nor more than three miles from the great valley road leading from Winchester to Abingdon, nor further north on the same than Woodstock, nor south than Fincastle, having reference in choosing a position on this line to the terms which any individual or association of individuals, body politic or corporate, may offer to them as an inducement to prefer any particular point: *provided,* that the lot of ground on which the public edifices of the University may be erected, shall not be less in extent than fifty acres. The board of public works shall design all the plans of the various edifices which may be erected thereupon, and contract for the building thereof; but no part thereof shall be begun until the lot aforesaid shall have been legally conveyed to the president and directors of the Literary Fund, nor until one hundred thousand dollars shall have been subscribed to defray the expense of the said buildings, and ten thousand dollars for the purchase of a library and philosophical apparatus for the said University. Such subscriptions may be of lands, stock or other property held in possession, reversion or remainder, and shall be, with all other subscriptions provided for by this act, made transferrable or payable to the president and directors of the Literary Fund, for such use as the subscribers shall severally make known at the time of subscribing.

XXV. *And be it further enacted,* That to develop the resources of the Commonwealth for the several objects provided for by this Act; the county and corporation courts within the same, are authorized and required to appoint at their next March term three or more commissioners from among the most industrious and patriotic citizens within their respective counties and corporations, to make personal application to all the inhabitants thereof for subscriptions towards the establishment of the primary schools, academies, colleges and university proposed to be created under this Act. The commissioners shall return the original subscription lists to their respective county or corporation courts, and a certified copy thereof to the President and Directors of the Literary Fund: who shall cause their secretary to make proper abstracts therefrom, showing the amount subscribed to each of the objects aforesaid, and the names of the several subscribers, and the sums respectively subscribed by them; a copy of which abstracts he shall transmit to the Board of Public Instruction for the information thereof. In the minutes of the proceedings of the Board of Public Instruction, and of the trustees of the several colleges, academies and primary schools, the names of the subscribers to the foundation thereof shall be carefully inscribed with the sums subscribed by each opposite thereto, as a perpetual memorial of the persons who shall have contributed to promote the diffusion of knowledge throughout the Commonwealth.

XXVI. *And be it further enacted,* That the trustees of all the primary schools, Academies and Colleges, shall annually by the first day of August of each year report to the Board of Public Instruction the actual condition of their respective schools, academies and colleges. In these reports, the name of the school derived from the township or ward; of the academy with the number of the academical districts in which it is situated; and of the college, shall be denoted, also the number and denomination of the teachers or professors, the number and ages of the pupils or students in such school, academy or college, the extent of the library, if any, attached thereto, the cost or value, and state of repair of the several edifices devoted to literature, and such other general remarks as may serve to show the progress or declension of the several primary schools, academies, and colleges. Out of these reports, the Board of Public Instruction shall annually compile, and submit to the General Assembly, at, or near the commencement of their annual session, a view of the state of public education, within the Commonwealth, embracing a history of the progress, or declension of the University of Virginia in the year next preceding and illustrating its actual condition and future prospects.

XXVII. *And be it further enacted,* That the President and Directors of the Literary Fund shall continue, as heretofore, under the protection of the General Assembly, the depositary and guardian of that fund, and to them all conveyances shall be made of property presented to or purchased for the use of the Literary Fund.

XXVIII. *And be it further enacted,* That all acts and parts of acts coming within the purview of this act, shall be, and the same are hereby repealed.

XXIX. This act shall commence and be in force from and after the passage thereof.

[Mercer adds the following comment to his bill as it was printed in the Appendix to his speech. It is a generous appeal to the citizens of Virginia to rally behind the University which his opponent Jefferson had established.

The part of the former resolution, denominating and providing for the erection of the University of Virginia, has been since executed; at such cost, however, to the literary fund of the state, as to impair, very much, its ability to sustain a system of primary schools, coextensive with the territory and the wants of the commonwealth. Whatever errors may have been committed in the location of the university, and in the structure of its edifices, should give place to zeal for its ultimate success in which every state of this union has an interest as well as Virginia. To the other parts of the present system for her elementary instruction, a hope may be rationally indulged, that when time shall disclose their defects, the wisdom of her legislature will not be backward in devising for them suitable remedies.]

Index